the practical spinner's guide

Cotton, Flax, Her

Stephenie Gaustad

JUL -- 2014

D1191611

INTERWEAVE.
interweave.com

BELLEVILLE PUBLIC LIBRARY

EDITORS
Ann Budd, Linda Ligon

ASSOCIATE ART DIRECTOR
Julia Boyles

PROJECT & SAMPLE PHOTOGRAPHER
Joe Coca

**PHOTO STYLIST &
STEP-BY-STEP PHOTOGRAPHER**
Ann Swanson

COVER & INTERIOR DESIGN
Adrian Newman

ILLUSTRATIONS
Stephenie Gaustad

PRODUCTION
Katherine Jackson

© 2014 Stephenie Gaustad
Photography © 2014 Interweave
Illustrations © 2014 Stephenie Gaustad
All rights reserved.

Interweave
A division of F+W Media, Inc.
201 East Fourth Street
Loveland, CO 80537
interweave.com

Manufactured in China by RR Donnelley Shenzhen

Library of Congress Cataloging-in-Publication Data

Gaustad, Stephenie.

 The practical spinner's guide : cotton, flax, hemp /
Stephenie Gaustad.

   pages cm

 Includes index.

ISBN 978-1-59668-669-4 (pbk)
ISBN 978-1-59668-986-2 (PDF)

1. Hand spinning. I. Title.

TT847.G38 2014

746.1'2--dc23

                2013025629

10 9 8 7 6 5 4 3 2 1

Acknowledgments

This book is in your hands because a number of people opened doors for me. Well before easy internet research, trail-breakers Bette Hochberg and Olive and Harry Lindner wrote and published works on plant fibers. Linda Ligon listened to my ideas, saw my enthusiasm, and helped me realize the book "in there." My greatest debt is owed to my mentor, partner, husband, and friend, Alden Amos.

Dedication

This book is dedicated to spinning students everywhere.

TABLE *of* CONTENTS

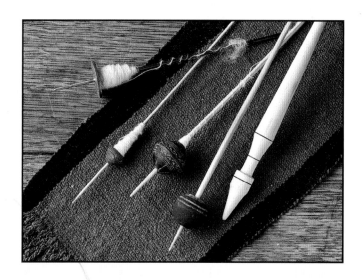

Foreword

LIKE STEPHANIE GAUSTAD, I have a long, ongoing love affair with fiber. Also like Stephenie, I have been immersed in fiber my whole life. I have worked with the animals, grown the plants, processed, spun, dyed, woven, and knitted. I have written, talked, and filmed. But it's still a chilly moment, at the party or on the plane, when someone turns to me and asks, "And just what is it that you do?" I used to fudge and say, "Well, I teach." But inevitably, the next question would be "What do you teach?" And when I would answer "textiles," they would say, "Oh, you must knit sweaters." Although I never learned to dodge the initial question, I have learned to take refuge in my favorite fantasy at moments like that. I just imagine the Good Wish Fairy fluttering by, granting me one wish. I'd wish that all textiles on the face of the earth would vanish, not forever, but just for a day, perhaps two, maybe a week. Just long enough to make people grateful for the amazing accumulation of knowledge that lets us continue to create the threads of our lives. It wouldn't be long before the path to my door and yours, dear reader, would be trodden flat by hordes of shivering, naked people asking, "Aren't you the one who does that funny thing with string?"

It would be a cold, dark, and hungry world without thread. And if, wickedly, I expanded my wish just a tiny little bit to include all technologies that have arisen directly from the field of textiles—which would include ceramics, the computer, and the engineering that made the Golden Gate Bridge—no one would be unaffected, except chickadees (they've been around for millions of years) and fireflies. Back in time, the occasional humanoid might lift his head in puzzlement as the thigh-spun sinew cord disappeared from his wooden spear shaft, dropping the stone spearhead to the cave floor. Ah, there went dinner.

Another chilling question, as any of you who have bravely spun in public know well, is "Why do you spin?" Consider just how useful it is for humans to have clothes that can be conveniently changed at the whim of the weather, not to mention all the nonclothing things that don't work without the input of textiles—refrigerators, cars, furnaces, hospitals, and paper, for a tiny start. Surely the properly defiant answer is "Why on earth do you not?" (even though I realize that machines do much of this for us now).

I've heard many answers to the why-spin question over the years. My friend and business partner for many years came from Sámi ancestors. Pavii's father's family were nomadic reindeer herders who traveled on their yearly migration across Finland and into Russia on foot. During the terrible influenza epidemic in the early 1900s, his entire tribe, except himself and his older brother, perished in the middle of the wilderness. The two young boys, not even teenagers, walked alone for months to Russia, where they were rescued and adopted by a Russian family. Raised to never forget what it was to be self-reliant, Pavii is a brilliant spinner and weaver; she designs software equally well. When I asked her why she wanted to spin, she answered, "Because we are always only a week away from the tent."

I think the answer that has the most resonance for me came from a student I had many years ago in Canada. One of the original European designers of the solar cell, he had retired to Vancouver Island, off the coast of British Columbia, where he and his wife built a house. Their house was entirely powered by solar energy, with one exception: they chose to light their house with beeswax candles made with wax collected from their own bees. It was an unforgettable experience to spend an evening with them in their beautiful, luminous house. He took many classes with me—spinning, weaving, papermaking, dyeing, felting. I was curious why someone whose whole career had been involved in developing state-of-the-art technology would be so interested in methods that appear both simple and ancient. This is his answer: "I want to demystify technology. I want to understand what I am asking a machine to do for me; I want to know what I gain and what I lose when I choose to use a machine rather than doing something by hand. And then, I want to choose." Like this man, I want to know the cost—personally, environmentally, socially—of the decisions I make on how I live in the world.

Here is a good example of what I know from asking myself the question "Why spin?" I have loved weaving my handspun sauna towels,

and it gives me much pleasure to use them in my day-to-day life. On the other hand, I am eternally grateful that there are cotton mills to spin the exquisitely fine cotton that was machine woven into the bedsheets that I sleep under every night. I do get to choose.

I learned to spin from Mrs. Axen, a woman who had simply chosen spinning as her way of being in the world. As soon as I saw a spinning wheel, my fingers made their own decision— and she understood that. Mrs. Axen spun flax beautifully and wove all her tea towels and bed linens. She washed wool from lamb fleeces and dried them on her lilac bushes to make the best mitts and socks in my known world. She wove and sewed the beautiful long dresses she wore. Stephenie reminds me so much of her, and not just because they look alike—which they very much do—but because their way of being in this world includes the same deep integrity and the same calm competence. I have a friend who, like so many of us, was struck speechless when she realized that when Stephenie said she had made the shirt she was wearing not only, as my friend assumed, had she sewn it, but she had also woven the cloth. As my friend

a snake." The yarn was dreadful, harsh and brittle, not at all what she had envisioned.

Stephenie speaks for all of us—weavers, spinners, knitters, and lovers of cloth alike—when she says that what's available in the marketplace today is a thin shadow of the true potential of textiles. How can what is available for purchase be the best fabric and thread those twenty thousand years of work and study could bring us? She is perfectly correct in saying that it is not. We, who work with our hands, know better. Have a look at the fragments of Nazca cotton fabric from Peru spun a couple of thousand years ago with a stone and a bit of stick. You can't count the number of plies without a microscope. These threads, woven into intricate gauze and complex lace patterns, are also strong enough to have survived into our time, filling us with wonder at their complex beauty. The cost of relying on a machine is often excellence. Sometimes, as is true of my bedsheets, that cost is reasonable. However, when you see (and touch) Stephenie's handspun, handwoven fabric or a bit of Nazca cloth, you realize that there are times, even in this modern world—or perhaps especially in this modern world—that the cost we pay for mechanized production is fiercely high. And, in truth, as Pavii would say, we're not all that far from the tent.

recovered from her first amazement, she had to come to terms with the fact that Stephenie had also spun the exquisite fine thread the cloth had been woven from. And before that, Stephenie had planted, watered, nurtured, and harvested the cotton that she spun into that exquisite fine thread.

I recently asked Stephenie the "Why spin" question. As we looked at some of her beautiful, floating-like-a-cloud cotton fabric, she said, "Honey, if I could buy it, I would. I'm in it for the yarn!" Although she finds the process of spinning delightful and easy to give her time to, she spins because of "the huge difference in quality between what I can make and what I can buy." She told me the story of how as a young weaver she went into a yarn store and saw a beautiful yarn across the crowded room. It was a love-at-first-sight moment. She said the yarn was gorgeous, red and luscious. When she rushed over to pick it up, she said, "I recoiled as if I'd been bitten by

This is especially true when you look at cotton, the fiber staple of American life and a fiber that Stephenie, as a teacher of spinning and weaving, has devoted much of her life to. As she would tell you, the history of this country is intimately tied to the history of cotton. Several years ago, I read Laurel Thatcher Ulrich's Pulitzer–prizewinning book *A Midwife's Tale: the Life of Martha Ballard*. If you love textiles and history, you should read this book. Martha Ballard was born in 1735 in Oxford, Massachusetts, before the Revolution. She was born before cotton mills, and she was born before the cotton gin was invented. The book is a record of her life as a midwife, as a spinner, and as a weaver. The entry in the diary that I found so riveting was, for her, an ordinary day.

She and her little dog row her boat along the sound to do the rounds of her patients. She is fighting a scarlet fever outbreak, armed with the herbs and tinctures she makes from her garden. It's a wearying day for her, full of concern for the elderly and the children she has delivered. But when she comes home, she sits down to her wheel to finish 27 yards of sturdy linen thread so that tomorrow the village shoemaker will be able to make shoes. Martha died in 1812, two hundred years ago. Also in 1812, Coats and Clarke introduced the first commercial cotton sewing thread. Not even an eyeblink ago in the long history of textile development, you and I would have been looking for Stephenie, our clothes in tatters and our ragged-soled shoes tucked under our arms.

Stephenie is quite clear that whether the yarn was spun by state-of-the-art, computer-driven textile machinery, elves in the Black Forest, or herself, it's the quality of the thread that she looks for. She makes yarn to use, and she has made sure, through study and practice, that she has the skills she needs to achieve thread that will meet her standards. I'm sure one of the virtual signs hanging in her studio is "Perfect Will Be Good Enough."

I looked up the word "practical" in the Oxford Concise Dictionary. The word comes from the Greek word *praktikos*, meaning concerned with action. The dictionary included these definitions: "concerned with doing or use of something rather than with theory or ideas; suitable for a particular purpose; likely to succeed or be effective in real circumstances and (of a person) sensible and realistic in their approach to a situation or problem."

Like Mrs. Axen a generation before her, Stephenie is a most practical woman. She is also a witness to a road not taken by the mainstream world. Machines can only do what we ask them to do. In this modern world of textile excess and waste, we ask them to do less and less. We seem to have settled for just "Good Enough." In writing this book, Stephenie has condensed and refined years of research and study about cellulose fibers, as well as years of work in the garden, at the spinning wheel, and at her loom. This practical work, guided by a mind that asks "What if," an eye that's diligent, and a hand that's gifted, will give Pavii, and the rest of us, the information we need to continue to make the thread of our dreams.

—Judith MacKenzie

CHAPTER ONE:

Cotton

When cotton was first introduced to Europeans in medieval times, they were mystified. What was the source of this marvelous material? Theories abounded. For a time, the source was thought to be "the Vegetable Lamb of Tartary"—a plant with tiny sheep on stems bowing down and grazing the undergrowth. One can only imagine how they thought all those tiny sheep were shorn.

Cotton Species

'VARIOUS SPECIES OF COTTON had been cultivated across Asia, Mexico, and South America for thousands of years before the "vegetable lamb" botanical confusion arose; traces of their fibers have been discovered in woven fragments that attest to their broad use and antiquity. Cotton, *Gossypium spp.*, is a member of the Malvaceae, or mallow, family, a relative of hibiscus, hollyhocks, and okra. It has four main species: *Gossypium hirsutum, G. barbadense, G.herbaceum,* and *G. arboreum.*

HERBACEUM is sometimes found imported from India. It's quite coarse and has a very short staple of $5/8$" (1.5 cm).

BARBADENSE can have a much greater staple length of $1^{1}/2$" to 2" (3.8 to 4 cm). It's a very fine fiber and includes Pima, Sea Island, and some "Egyptian" cottons.

HIRSUTUM (also known as "Upland" cotton), with a staple length of around 1" to $1^{1}/4$" (2.5 to 3.2 cm), is the cotton most commonly grown worldwide.

ARBOREUM is a tree cotton, native to the Indian subcontinent. *Arboreum* fiber is rare, and virtually never available to spinners in this country.

Most cotton on the global market is white, but cotton can occur in natural, nonwhite colors: rose, buff, brown, red, chocolate, green—even lilac, blue, and black.

From left to right: Herbaceum, Barbadense, and Hirsutum.

Cotton Fiber Characteristics

COTTON IS A SEED FIBER with many compelling qualities: it's soft, strong, cool to the touch, absorbent, and easily cleansed. It's stronger when wet, not harmed by temperatures well above boiling nor by alkaline soaps and detergents—all elements of a sanitary laundry. This fiber can be washed until clean, dries quickly, and doesn't attract moths.

Individual cotton fibers are fine, on a par with musk ox, cashmere, and merino wools. As noted above, they are also quite short, typically ranging from $5/8$" to $1\frac{1}{3}$" (1.5 cm to 3.5 cm) long. Of the textile plant fibers, cotton contains the highest percentage of cellulose: 95 percent. Flax, hemp, ramie, and the other plant fibers cannot boast this purity. The high percentage means that after repeated launderings, you'll only lose 5 percent, mostly waxes and oils that wash out of your yarn. Lacking the woody component of a stem fiber such as flax, cotton fiber is limp. This combination of small fiber diameter without stiffness gives cotton its natural softness. Despite their fineness, cotton fibers are strong—three times as strong as a typical wool fiber of the same diameter.

Cotton is comfortable in warm weather because it readily transfers heat away from the body. Combine that with its excellent moisture-wicking qualities, and you have a fiber that is soothing next to the skin—hence its popularity for underwear and lightweight summer garments. However, it's also used for blankets and outerwear, especially if it's fashioned into a fabric with a lot of insulative air spaces.

Every fiber has weak and strong points, and cotton is no exception. First, cotton isn't elastic like wool. Besides having a natural crimp, at the molecular level wool is coiled like a spring, giving it elasticity and the ability to recover its original shape. Cotton fiber, on the other hand, is made up of cells stacked like bricks with little or no elasticity in their structure. This lack of elasticity makes cotton tend to wrinkle and remain wrinkled.

Second, cotton won't felt or full. It won't bloom and fill in a woven or knitted structure as wool does. Laundering doesn't change the size of a cotton fabric much, except perhaps to temporarily shrink the diameter of a soft yarn. What is sometimes perceived as shrinkage in store-bought goods is actually relaxation or temporary finishes that have washed out. When it comes to handspun cotton, what comes off the loom or needles is pretty much what you get.

Third, mold and mildew destroy cotton. Just as microbes that prefer damp conditions damage paper, so bacteria and fungi attack cotton. Most remedies for mold and mildew involve application of an acid, which is likewise destructive to cellulose fibers. Rapid drying and dry storage will help to alleviate this problem, as will exposure to sunlight. All acids, even weak acids, damage cotton fibers, yarns, and textiles. Fruit juices, carbonated sodas, sugar, and even human perspiration can cause serious damage. Be sure to flush and rinse your cottons thoroughly with water when they come in contact with any acid.

Cotton burns at 451° F (233° C), another similarity to paper. It supports a flame and won't self-extinguish. In fact, it burns merrily and makes reasonable tinder.

As spinners, we're used to the way the scales on wool help it stick to itself and the way it feels as the scaly fibers slip past one another. So, if cotton has no scales, how does it hold together when you spin it? Let's consider how it grows to see what causes cotton fibers to stick to each other, and be spun into yarn.

Cotton fiber is the "hair" that covers the cotton seed. The cotton plant produces those seeds in a pod or "boll." As the boll develops, the naked seed begins to push out cells arranged to form tubes (which will become the fiber). These tubes have a "skin" and a core. Within a short time, the fiber tubes reach their full length. From then on, a new layer of cells is added daily to the core, thickening the tubes.

The hollow fibers are built somewhat like paper soda straws—strips of material that wind in a spiral. Unlike a soda straw, though, at certain points (called nodes), the strip of material reverses direction and spirals the other way. A single cotton fiber can have dozens of nodes along its length.

The boll enlarges and the cotton fibers mature and thicken until the boll begins to dry and crack. It splits open, curls back, and the cotton within puffs out to dry in the sun. As the fiber dries, the tubes collapse. Where a tube spiraled one direction, it twists in that same direction as it dries. At a node, where the tube spiraled in the opposite direction, the drying cotton fiber twists in that direction. In other words, the dry cotton fiber behaves as if it were a tape that twists one direction for a bit, then twists the other and back again. It is these twisted surfaces on each cotton fiber that attract and adhere to one another.

The fiber is hidden inside the unopened cotton bolls.

The enlarged boll splits open, curls back, and the fiber within puffs out to dry in the sun.

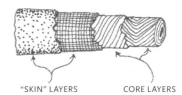

"SKIN" LAYERS   CORE LAYERS

Beneath the fiber skin, the core twists one direction, then reverses.

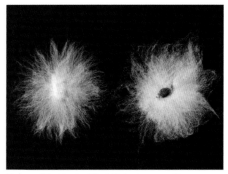

Cotton fiber is the "hair" that covers the cotton seed.

Growing Cotton

COTTON WILL GROW IN A WIDE range of climates. It was first introduced in China because its flower was beautiful, reason enough to have it in the garden. However, it produces bolls and good fiber in many areas where evening temperatures are warm. A rule of thumb is that if you can grow red tomatoes, then most likely you'll be able to grow cotton.

What Cotton Needs

Cotton, a perennial if there's no frost, but an annual if there is, needs a frost-free season of 180 to 220 days; full sun; and deep-tilled, well-manured, well-drained soil. Cotton has an extensive, deep root system, and young plants need attentive watering. As cotton matures, it becomes more drought tolerant. Set up an irrigation system that suits your soil so that the moisture reaches the deep tap roots. To protect against my dry, California clay/sand soil, I build a berm around each cotton plant, making a pan about 24" (61 cm) square. I flood the pan every two to three days as needed.

The soil must be warm before the seeds can germinate. Toward the middle of the season, the nights must also be warm for the cotton fruit, or bolls, to set.

Start with a good deep watering before you plant. When your soil is 58° F (14.5° C) at a depth of 1" (2.5 cm), plant your cotton at a depth of 1" (2.5 cm). Space the plants 36" to 48" (91.5 to 122 cm) apart. Germination will take place in six to ten days, with the seedling looking like that of a pea.

Pick the cotton as the bolls begin to dry and crack open. At first frost, you can pick unopened bolls and bring them indoors to dry and open. If the bolls freeze, oils in the husk will spoil the cotton fiber within.

At the end of the season, remove the plant debris from your beds. Many farmers burn the plants to return minerals to the soil and reduce insect populations the next year.

Harvesting Cotton

'IF YOU'RE FORTUNATE and can grow cotton in your backyard, then you can simply pick your cotton boll by boll as it cracks open and dries. In this manner, a minimum of dust and dirt collects on the cotton, and not much leaf trash is included in the picking. All cotton was picked by hand as recently as sixty years ago, but this handpicked, top grade has vanished since the introduction of mechanical harvesting.[1]

In this country, virtually all large-scale commercially produced cotton is harvested by machine. This method is efficient and, in the long run, less expensive for the grower. But for the person who buys the fiber and spins it, several things inherent in the harvesting process complicate the job.

First, cotton fields are treated with chemicals that cause the plant's leaves to dry up and the bolls to crack all at once so that the harvesting equipment can move in to do its job on schedule. A chemical residue remains on the cotton fiber of bolls that were open when the chemicals were applied. (Organic farmers don't use chemical defoliants, pesticides, or fertilizers, so their harvest is especially desirable for handspinners.)

Second, mechanically harvested cotton includes some dried leaf and plant bits known as "leaf trash." Most of this trash is removed by the seed-removal or "ginning" process. Big blowers move the cotton through the process and separate out a good deal of the trash. Really trashy cotton, however, can't be

Bits of leaf trash are visible in this cotton sample.

thoroughly cleaned by the ginning process. You can see bits of hull and leaf as tiny black spots in unbleached muslin. Bits of hull and leaf left in white cotton will ultimately dye it a manila color.

Mechanical harvesting also can cause fibers to tangle and form "neps." Like "pills" in our knitting, neps are broken fibers that are swirled into knots by abrasion. The fiber breaks for many reasons: immaturity, moisture, and insect attack, to name a few. Of course, introduction of excessive plant material and neps could be reduced by good field and picking management—or by doing it yourself.

---

1 Machine harvesting introduces more leaf trash than does hand picking. This premium grade was known as "middling fair" and still exists in our language as the phrase "fair to middling" as a statement of status.

Preparing Cotton Fiber

'BEFORE YOU SIT DOWN TO SPIN prepared cotton, it can be really helpful to understand the steps that have been taken to get the fiber organized and in condition to spin. Then again, you may decide to do the preparation yourself, because fiber that has been skillfully prepared by hand is superior to any you can purchase. Either way, it's good to understand the fundamental processes.

Removing the Seeds

A freshly picked boll of cotton is full of seeds that must be removed before any further fiber preparation begins. Aside from getting seriously in the way if you try to spin before de-seeding,[2] the seeds present other liabilities. They are full of oil that can contaminate the surrounding fiber and make it impossible to gin or spin. In warm locations with high humidity, large piles of seed cotton can even catch fire!

Cotton seeds can be removed by hand, but the process is exceedingly slow. Sometimes the fiber, or lint, slips off the seed with a gentle pull. At other times, a firm grip and pull is not enough to get it all free.

If you've had the opportunity to de-seed cotton by hand, you may have discovered that not all cotton seeds are alike. They're of two general types: hairy-seeded and slick- or smooth-seeded. When the longer fibers are pulled off hairy-seeded cotton, a short, dense fuzz remains, leaving the seeds looking like tiny furry bears. Slick seeds, on the other

*A short dense fuzz remains after the the longer fibers have been pulled off **hairy-seeded cotton seeds** (left). **Slick-seeded cotton seeds** (right) release the fiber easily.*

An early form of gin consists of a steel pin that rolls across a flat surface; it's best used for slick-seeded cotton.

hand, release their fiber easily and have little to no fiber left on them—perhaps just a tuft on one end. The two seed types need distinctly different tools for removal.

Single- and Dual-Roller Gins

"Ginning" is the term for removing the seed by "gin," a name that derives from "engine." Gins can be small simple devices or massive complex mechanisms housed in warehouse-sized buildings. (Don't worry, we'll get to Eli Whitney.) An early form of gin consists of nothing more than a steel pin that rolls across a flat surface. A small wad of seed cotton is put on a stone slab with the pin just touching the edge of the clump of cotton. The pin is rolled across the mass of

---

2 It is possible to spin cotton directly off the seed. Although it's not a productive or high-speed process, it does make a good show.

seed cotton with a firm downward pressure that pulls fibers off the seeds and pushes the seeds in front of the roller to drop over the edge of the slab. Gins of this type have been in use for centuries, but they only work well with slick-seeded cottons such as Pima, Sea Island, and Egyptian types.

A more sophisticated and productive version consists of two rollers that nearly touch, set in a frame that permits them to counter rotate—think of wringer washer rollers or a pasta machine. When cotton is fed into the roller gin, the fibers squeak through, but the seeds cannot. This kind of roller gin is also most effective with the slick-seeded cottons.

Although you can gin hairy-seeded cotton with a roller gin, the process is neither fast nor efficient. Individual seeds may not release all their fibers, causing these seeds to jam in the rollers, get crushed, release oil, and contaminate the fiber. In short, it forms a big mess! The process is finicky, requires skill, and certainly isn't acceptable for industrial needs.

Eli Whitney's Gin

Another gin design solved this problem. This type of gin sets the seed cotton in a hopper, where it contacts rotating saw blades. The saw blades draw the fiber off the seed and behind a grate through which the seeds can't pass. The blades are swept clean by brushes, and the cotton fiber and the seeds fall down separate chutes. Eli Whitney developed, took credit for, and patented this gin design in 1794. (He claims to have gotten the idea from watching his cat swipe at a bird through a picket fence.)

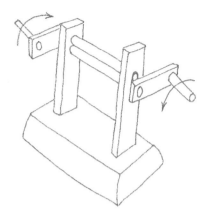

A roller gin is also most effective on slick-seeded cotton.

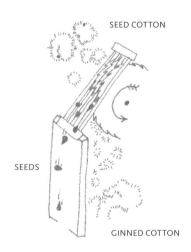

SEED COTTON

SEEDS

GINNED COTTON

Eli Whitney's gin works well on hairy-seeded cotton.

Roller-ginned cotton can condense into ropy masses that are tricky to card.

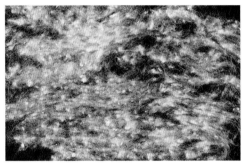

Saw-ginned cotton can have irregular staple lengths and abundant nepps.

How Ginning Affects Cotton Fiber

So, why should the ordinary handspinner be concerned with cotton gins? The type of gin that has been used can affect the quality of the fiber, ease of carding and spinning, and, ultimately, the quality of your yarn. Unless you get your fibers straight from the gin, do your own ginning, or buy uncarded cotton, the ginned fiber condition may not be obvious. Let's take a closer look.

Long, fine cottons are often slick-seeded and ginned with a roller gin. Because the rollers compress the fibers, the condensed soft fibers can turn "ropy," making the cotton tricky to card. Severely ropy fibers are entangled and, as you card them, the fibers tear, producing irregular staple lengths and neps (torn, short fibers that ball up during carding into soft—or not so soft—knots).

Saw-ginned cotton can also be neppy, but for a different reason. Because hairy-seeded cottons are ginned by saw blades, fibers can become snagged, torn, and tangled. Once carded into the fiber preparation, these neps can be removed only by picking them out. One by one.

In other words, roller-ginned fiber doesn't start out full of neps. If the fibers are condensed into ropes, it becomes neppy as you card it. Saw-ginned fiber can start out nepped, and no amount of carding can remove the neps.

Neps are a serious fault. As you're spinning, the fiber can't readily flow past and around all the "knots," and the yarn won't be smooth and even. Perhaps you don't want your yarn to look too smooth and even? Never fear. Cotton that has been spun by hand will have an unmistakable character—and can be superior to machine-spun cotton.

Willowing

Because cotton is so easily compressed and doesn't spring back, you can't manually tease the fiber open as you would wool. The more you attempt to open it up, the denser it becomes. You need to use a hands-free technique. Willowing is such a technique—ancient and ubiquitous throughout many of the cotton-growing parts of the world.

Willowing is a fiber-opening technique that consists of fluffing the fiber with a pair of wands while the fiber rests on a screen. The open mesh of the screen permits trash and soil to fall through the grid, cleaning the fiber while the denser areas of the fiber are opened and randomized. It is akin to beating egg whites into meringue, only with an "up-and-down" instead of a "round-and-round" movement.

To try out this process, you'll need a screen with large holes (½" [1.3 cm] square), some way to get the screen up in the air at about hip height, and two sapling suckers (willow withes were traditionally used in England; hence the term "willowing"). You can substitute ¼" (6 mm) dowels about 30" (76 cm) long if you don't have any flexible branches handy. You'll also need a sense of humor and patience.

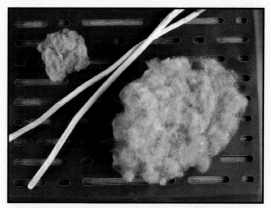

In willowing, a **mass of cotton fiber** (upper left) is fluffed with a pair of sticks to remove trash and **open up the fibers** (lower right).

Place the cotton to be willowed in the center of the screen. What you're going to do is whap the pile of cotton with one stick, then whap it again with the other stick. The goal is to lift the cotton into the air, fluff and open it, and cause the trash to fall out.

Like all spinning-related tasks, willowing is a skill. Doing it over and over again will improve your results. It also helps if the cotton is this year's crop (see tips for carding cotton on page 23). Well-willowed cotton looks like a cloud.[3]

---

3 Some First Americans of the Southwestern U.S. believe that cotton is life-giving rain clouds come to earth, and is evidence of the covenant between the people and their maker.

CARDING COTTON

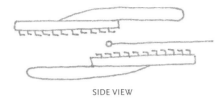

SIDE VIEW

Carding occurs in the small space between the cards.

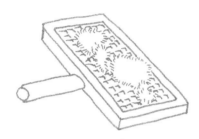

Place open fiber on one handcard held in your dominant hand.

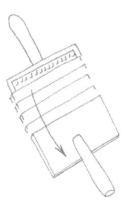

Wipe the dominant handcard close above the other card without touching the teeth.

Carding

Like wool, cotton can be carded, but the tools are somewhat different. Cotton handcards have finer wires that are set closer together and bent to a different angle. Can you use wool handcards for cotton? If they're pristine, perhaps. If they have any fiber on them, you're asking for trouble. Clean them. Vacuum them. If you have used them to card greasy fleece, "all hope abandon."

Carding occurs in the small space between the face of each card as one card passes the other without ever touching. The fiber in that working space is opened and organized as the card wires pass over it. Any cotton below the tips of the wires is out of range and won't be affected. If the wire tips contact fiber beneath the tips and each other, the result is fiber breakage. The message: lay the fiber lightly on the surface of the card and pass the cards gently across each other without actually touching. It's a delicate operation.

To begin, place a bit of open fiber on one hand card. Hold that card in your nondominant hand with the handle pointing away from your body. Hold the second card by the handle with the teeth pointing to the floor. (The handles of the card oppose one another when you're working the fiber.)

Use a wiping motion to pass the dominant-hand card close to, but not touching, the other card. Fiber will collect on one card, at which point it needs to be transferred to the other card so that the other side of the cotton "batt" or "lap" can be addressed.

 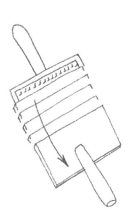  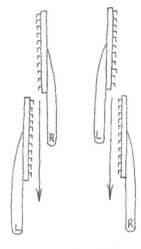

To transfer from the left to the right card, wipe the right card down the left.

Wipe the dominant-handcard close above the other one.

To transfer from the right to the left, wipe the left card down the right.

To remove the carded lap, transfer it to the right, then to the left, lifting the fiber off both.

To transfer from one card to the other, hold a card in each hand, with the handles pointing down and the wiry part of the cards facing one another. Lower one card so that the top edge (the "toe") of it is even with the bottom edge (the "heel") of the other card. Wipe the lower card across the other one with an upward movement, being careful not to engage the teeth of either card. Transfer the fiber from your left handcard to the right handcard, and then right to left to card both sides of the cotton. Transfer the fiber from one card to the other until the lap has no streaks, is open, and the fibers are evenly distributed. To remove the carded lap, transfer it to the right, then transfer it to the left, lifting the carded fiber off both handcards.

Tips for Carding Cotton

❀ Because cotton is a fine fiber, it's easy to overload the cards. Load what may seem to you to be a measly amount on the carders. You can always put more fiber on the next lap as you become accustomed to the way that cotton cards.

❀ Fresh cotton is easiest to card well. As soon as the boll opens, the cotton begins to dry out. In addition to seeds, raw cotton contains waxy oils that oxidize in time, forming gummy compounds on the fiber surface. These compounds make the fiber difficult to open up, become organized, and release soil and leaf trash. You can still card cotton that is "elderly," however, if you take time to open it up by willowing before you card.

❀ Don't engage the teeth of the carder while you card. Remember that the steel wire in the card clothing is stronger than the cotton fiber you're working to arrange. You can easily tear the cotton fibers. Torn fibers turn into neps.

❀ Stop carding when you see neps form. Fibers tear and turn into neps for many reasons. Static is a major one. When you hand-card cotton, you don't have many options to reduce static charge. Increased humidity is helpful. Don't card on a day when the north wind blows and humidity is in the single digits. If necessary, you can condition the fiber in a steamy bathroom for an hour or two. Once neps begin to form, they will continue to form at an increasing pace. Stop when you see the first ones.

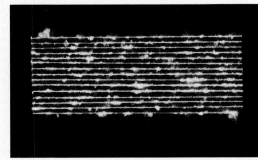

Neps formed in carding will present themselves in the spun yarn.

Cotton rolags are very soft and will easily smear on clothing.

Making Rolags

Wool spinners make a rolag from the lap that comes off the handcard. They transfer the fiber to one card and then transfer it back. The lap sits on the surface of the card clothing and is easily rolled up into a soft cylinder. This fiber form works well in wool, but not so well with cotton. It's very difficult to maintain the organization of cotton rolags unless you protect and cover them. Stow them away in a sturdy box or tin. You don't want to spoil your good effort only to discover the rolag smeared across the hem of your skirt or slacks.

Making Punis

A far more durable fiber form is the puni. If rolags are like woolen "pastries," punis are cotton "cigars." Instead of being light and fluffy, punis are dense. Punis use cotton's natural tendency to compress to govern the flow of fibers.

To make a puni, you'll need some willowed or handcarded fiber, a smooth stick, dowel, or knitting needle with a point at each end.

To begin, place your carded fiber on a smooth surface.

Place the stick along one edge of the fiber mass and roll the fiber mass onto the stick. Think of rolling up a piece of paper into a tube around a pencil.

Continuing in the same direction, give an additional roll with the palm of your hand. (Resist the impulse to roll back and forth as if you're making clay snakes. That doesn't work.)

Grab the end of the stick, and slide the puni off. Voilà! Your first puni!

Before you get carried away making punis, try spinning one. If it doesn't draft well, make another with less pressure. If it comes out too freely, make the next puni with more pressure on the final roll. Each new source of raw cotton may require that you adjust how you make your punis. Do a trial spin and modify your working pressure for each batch.

MAKING A PUNI

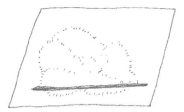

Place a smooth stick at the edge of the fiber.

Roll the fibers onto the stick.

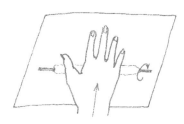

Give a last roll with your hand.

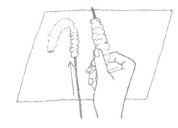

Pop the fiber off the end of the stick.

Using Prepared Fiber

You certainly don't have to do all the preparation yourself. Cotton can be purchased in many forms—as batts, punis, sliver, and roving—carded, organized, and ready to spin.

Occasionally, you can find cotton fiber in **batt** form—a large carded lap that looks like a pillow. Peel off a sheer layer and roll it up into a long "rolag" to see if it works for you as is. You can always recard it if it doesn't work. You can also make your own batts from your handcarded cotton by laying one unrolled lap off the handcards upon another until you build up your own batt. The advantage to making a larger fiber form is that doing so helps to homogenize the fiber qualities and color if there's variation.

Cotton is most commonly spun from batts, punis, sliver, and roving.

A cotton batt looks like a soft pillow.

To make your own batt, stack laps as they come off your handcarders.

Sliver is either carded or combed. In carded sliver, the staple length is random, as is the fiber orientation. Be aware that a mixture of staple lengths will produce slubs in your yarn. Combed sliver, or "top," is of a uniform staple length, and the fibers are as parallel as possible. Having a consistent staple length can produce the most consistent yarn.

Roving is a miniature sliver about the diameter of a small pencil, and therefore is often called "pencil roving." Cotton fiber that's already drafted down into this smaller form makes for a quick spin. Just be careful not to squash it between your thumb and forefinger.

Like all machine-prepared forms, there's a "good" and a "better" end from which to spin a sliver or roving. This is because the fibers were laid on one another in sequence, much like shingles on a roof. Spinning from the proper end of the sliver lets fibers flow with their original orientation. The yarn will have a smoother surface and no "slubs of unusual size." Going "against the grain" produces yarn with a hairy surface and exaggerated slubs. How do you know which end is the better one? Try one and then turn the sliver or roving around and spin from the other. You'll experience the difference.

Handle the sliver as little as possible, being aware that if you compress it even casually, it won't spin well. Cotton does not respond nicely to pressure of any kind. Treat it like a delicate living creature.

A serious note: After decades of spinning, it's clear to me that if you attend to the details of fiber prep, you'll be paid off with more and better yarn in significantly less time.

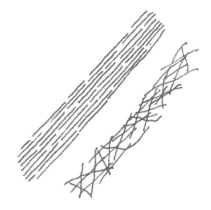

Combed sliver *(left) has parallel orientation while* **carded sliver** *(right) has random orientation.*

Roving *(left) is a miniature* **sliver** *(right) that's about the diameter of a small pencil.*

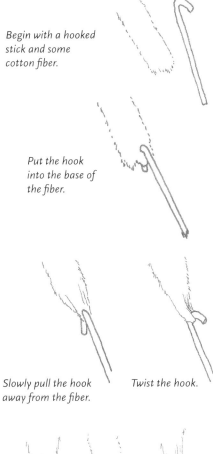

*Begin with a hooked
stick and some
cotton fiber.*

*Put the hook
into the base of
the fiber.*

*Slowly pull the hook
away from the fiber.*

Twist the hook.

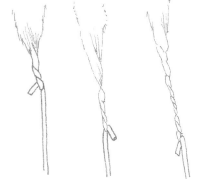

Continue to pull and twist.

Spinning Cotton

ONE OF THE MOST INFLUENTIAL spinners of recent times, Bette Hochberg, once said, "Of all the fibers spun over the past 20,000 years, the one that has clothed, protected, and warmed the greatest number of people is cotton." Yet such a significant fiber has a rather sad reputation among contemporary handspinners. Cotton is said to be difficult to spin. Is that so? Well, not if you take its characteristics into consideration and handle it accordingly—most likely in a manner that will seem unfamiliar if you're accustomed to spinning wool.

The Mechanics of Spinning Cotton

Let's experience those fiber characteristics first hand. You'll need some prepared fiber in puni, sliver, or roving form and a hooked stick made from a coat hanger or wire (in a pinch, you can use the threading hook from your spinning wheel).

Hold the fiber in one hand and the hooked stick in the other. Use the hook to slowly catch a few fibers—a very few fibers. Keep the hook steady and don't let it wander from side to side, but keep it rotating at the same point in space. Next, pull the hook hand slowly away from the fiber hand. This is called "drafting" the fiber.

If you pull at just the right rate, and twist at just the right rate, you'll draft out a soft, barely spun tuft of cotton fiber. You're beginning to make something known as "slubbing." It isn't yarn yet and will drift apart if you pull on it. It's actually a form of lightly twisted roving. The important thing is that you get the sense of the cotton fiber sliding against itself and oozing into a soft "almost" yarn.

If you put the hook in the fiber and twist, but instead of drafting, you have to tug to get just a tightly twisted tapered tail, you have too much twist. Unhook the fiber, pull off the twisted bit and start over. Use less twist before you pull.

If you put the hook in the fiber and twist, but the fiber just drifts apart and won't stay on the hook, you probably don't have enough twist. Or you're pulling too far. Unhook the fiber, pull off the barely twisted bit, and start over. Put the hook a little deeper into the fiber mass next time and put in just a bit more twist—a quarter- or half-turn—before you begin pulling.

As you work with the fiber, eventually you'll be able to draft out a soft, barely spun "yarn." Practice until you've gotten a sense of what it takes to produce 10" (25.5 cm) of this lightly spun yarn. What you're experiencing is a primary characteristic of the cotton fiber: it has a lot of affinity for itself. It drafts easily with little twist.

If you've already tried to add twist to this "ghost yarn" to make it stronger, you've discovered that drafting after adding twist is difficult to impossible. Or the yarn gets suddenly really fat. This is the second significant characteristic of cotton fiber: if there's enough twist to make it a yarn, it's too much twist to allow the fiber to draft the next time you pull on it.

So put down the hooked stick and listen up.

The real secret to spinning cotton lies in managing two opposing factors: a little twist will permit the fiber to be drawn out, but enough twist to make a yarn is too much twist to allow the next bit to be drawn out.

So it would appear that cotton is sensitive to twist. But the real story is that cotton is soft and easily compressed. It wrinkles readily at the individual fiber level. The wrinkles won't open up and relax, as wool fibers do. Wool forgives a myriad of insults because it's elastic and has good elastic recovery. You can squash a wool rolag, and it will pop back like a cartoon hero. Once cotton fibers are wrinkled, on the other hand, their adhesive quality comes into play. Fluffy cotton turns into an unusable wad, even when casually squished. As soon as the fibers are wrinkled, their adhesive quality increases and the fibers can no longer slip or slide past one another. Once compressed by being twisted together, the fibers are locked.

One approach to spinning cotton starts with drawing the fibers out into a soft, barely-spun thread, then adding twist to that section of forming yarn while extending and lengthening it to stretch out the slubs. This process is called a "two-stage draft." During the drafting, the yarn can be lumpy and full of slubs, which is okay so long as the slubs aren't too hard or tightly twisted to draft out.

Twist is the mechanism that allows this lumpy yarn to be pulled smooth. Twist runs to the thin spots—in the way water pools in low-lying areas—and turns those thin spots into short lengths of solid yarn separated by loose slubs. As you extend the yarn, you can cause those slubs to thin out as you judiciously add twist. In this way, both ends of a slub are pulled and stretched, and ultimately transformed into sound yarn.

To see this in slow motion, get your hooked stick and do another draft, first to make soft slubs, and then to pinch off the yarn just below the drafting zone and pull the slubs smooth while adding twist. The way the twist moves into those slubs is lovely to see.

The "drafting zone" is the triangular area between the twist and the fiber mass in your hand. When you're drafting out fiber, the triangle should be visible. It's the same length as the staple, which, in cotton, is from ⅝" to 1⅓" (1.5 to 3.5 cm). In other words, it's short.

Pinch off the twist on the yarn just below the drafting zone to keep that twist out of the unspun fiber. Doing so lets you firm up the length of yarn without burying the twist in the fiber supply. Remember to hold the fiber with a light touch, taking care not to press your thumb onto the drafting zone.

You can go back to the hooked stick at any time to sample a new fiber or work through a problem. It is a great tool because everything involved with spinning—drafting and twisting—is slowed down so you can focus on the situation and see what's happening, and when. Every spinner's toolkit should include a hooked stick, along with an oil bottle, rag, and inch gauge.

As you draft, the yarn can be lumpy and full of slubs.

Extend the yarn to cause the slubs to thin out as you add twist.

The drafting triangle should be visible as you draft out the fiber.

Keep your thumb out of the drafting zone.

Essential Lessons

Spinning cotton presents a series of lessons. It teaches you to be scrupulous in your attention to twist. Not only do you need to be aware of how much twist you have, but also you need to know where that twist is—whether it's stalled at your lead hand, ganging up in thin areas, or evenly distributed throughout the length of the yarn. If you lose track of the twist, the easy graceful waltz of fiber flow turns into a spirited donnybrook.

Another significant lesson involves treating the spinning fiber with a light touch. Remember to hold the fiber lightly, taking care not to press your thumb onto the drafting zone. Don't clutch the fiber mass. I'm repeating this for emphasis because old habits are hard to break. What you have been able to get away with in spinning wool is utterly unworkable in cotton. If you compress your rolag, lap, batt, roving, sliver, or even puni, you set up a situation in which the fibers won't slip past each other easily. The result is yarn that's as irregular as a line of Morse Code (da, dit dit da, da dit).

Tools for Spinning Cotton

The hooked stick is nice, you may say, but your arm is tired and you want to go faster. Fortunately, you won't have to spin your wardrobe with the twisty stick. You can choose from many tools—spindles, treadled wheels, motor spinners, and charkhas all spin cotton.

But not all of them do it with the same speed and vigor. A cotton-spinning tool needs to do two things: deliver a fair amount of twist, and do so without much tug on the forming yarn. In other words, it has to produce lots of twist at a low rate of take up.

Spindles

Spindles were used exclusively in early cotton-growing and cotton-spinning cultures of the world: the highlands of South America and Mexico, the margins between ancient Persia and the Indian subcontinent, and the eastern Mediterranean (Levant). Characteristics of both handspindles and those driven with a drive wheel, such as the charkha, are that they lend themselves to a light and easy draft, fine yarn production with rapid twist, and measured and independent wind-on. In plain English, this means that there's no pull on the yarn while you're drafting it out, lots of twist when you need it, and easy control for winding onto bobbin or spindle. These spinning characteristics are what work on cotton. It makes sense that the tools that are most efficient would be found in those cultures where it has been spun most.

But can't tools from a flax or wool culture, like the treadled wheel or motor spinner, be used to spin cotton, too? Yes, if you can adjust them so that they permit a light and easy draft and combine rapid twist with gentle wind-on to produce a fine yarn.

Treadled Wheels

Let's begin with a familiar tool, the flyer-bobbin treadled wheel. I'm starting here, not because it's the best tool for the job, but because it may be the one with which you're most familiar. You'll need to make a few critical adjustments before you start, though. First, you need to adjust the wheel so you can use a light and easy draft, meaning little pull on the yarn as the wheel is putting in twist. The way to reduce take-up depends on the type of treadled wheel you use.

WAYS TO REDUCE TAKE-UP ON A SINGLE-DRIVE WHEEL

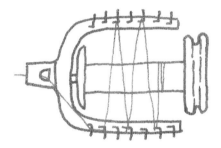

On a bobbin-led wheel, run the yarn back and forth between hooks on opposite sides of the flyer arm.

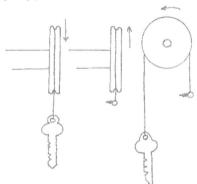

On a flyer-led wheel, replace the spring on the brake band with a key that dangles on the end of the band.

Single-Drive Wheels

If your wheel is a single-drive wheel (the drive cord is around the bobbin), you can attempt to reduce the take-up by running the yarn across a couple of hooks, bringing it to the other flyer arm and running it across a couple of hooks, and back and forth, and then out the orifice. Increasing friction on the yarn by threading it across the hooks in this way will diminish take-up, but it's only effective if the yarn is strong enough because it has plenty of twist. Unfortunately, if the flyer is large, as is often the case with this style of wheel, it can be slow to put in the twist, and it can be very difficult to make fine, high-twist cotton yarn.

It's easier to adjust the take-up on a single-drive wheel in which the drive cord is around the flyer. In this case, you reduce it by reducing tension on the bobbin brake. You can also replace the original brake band with a much finer one—even as fine as crochet cotton. The spring used to tension the brake band can be replaced by hanging a key on the end of the band and letting it dangle. To increase take-up, add more keys. Just take care that the keys don't get swept by the flyer or involved in any other nasty business with the drive wheel or treadle.

It helps if the bobbin is half-full before you begin, either with other yarn or wrapped with a foam cylinder, such as the ones used to insulate plumbing pipes.

Double-Drive Wheels

The double-drive wheel is a bit more complex because its take-up is governed by physical relationships between the flyer and bobbin whorls. To minimize take-up, you want both whorls to be close in size, with the flyer whorl just slightly larger than the bobbin. If you don't have this whorl set-up, you can try to increase slippage on the bobbin, either by reducing the overall drive cord tension, or by reducing the diameter of the drive cord, or both. A rule of thumb is to make the drive-cord diameter the same size as the yarn you wish to spin. (Be aware, though, that finer drive cords may require more tension, which can increase your treadling effort.)

You can take this procedure only so far. Let's say you have a heavy flyer with a giant whorl and a large bobbin with a somewhat smaller whorl. Putting a drive cord the size of sewing thread on this behemoth is unlikely to permit you to spin sewing thread. First of all, it will take you several treads just to get the flyer to turn over and get going. Then, when you get it up to speed, your twist insertion rate will be pretty poor because of wind resistance on the wheel and slippage on the drive cord. (However, it does make a great blower for those hot summer afternoons.)

Ideally, the flyer on a double-drive wheel for cotton spinning would be small (say a flyer length of 3" [7.5 cm]) and the drive wheel would be large (28" to 30" [71 to 76 cm]) for rapid twist insertion. Large, heavy flyers take effort to get going and, likewise, effort to stop (think of a large car). A lightweight flyer will behave more like a sports car—quick and responsive.

Adjusting for Plenty of Twist

The second requirement for spinning cotton is making a fine yarn with generous twist. Twist is produced when the bobbin and flyer, both driven by the wheel, rotate together. Some wheels have large drive wheels and some have compact ones. When it comes to making fine, high-twist yarn, it's better to have a wheel that puts in the twist quickly—that is, one with a high drive-wheel-to-flyer whorl ratio.

How to Determine Twist Ratio

Tie a piece of yarn to your flyer's arm for reference, then thread some yarn from the bobbin across the hooks and out the orifice. Hold on to the yarn coming out of the orifice.

Rotate the drive wheel one full revolution, counting the number of times the arm with the reference yarn goes round. Partial turns count.

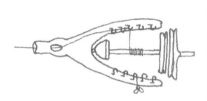

Tie yarn to the flyer arm and count the number of times it goes around with a single revolution of the drive wheel.

Most wheels' ratios fall between 3-to-1 and 25-to-1. In the first instance, for every single revolution of the drive wheel (or one tread), the flyer makes three turns (or puts roughly three turns in your yarn). Larger cotton yarns need five to seven turns per inch (2.5 cm) to hold together. This means that with a lower-ratio wheel, you may be pumping one tread to get 1" (2.5 cm) of yarn. It also means that your knee, ankle, and foot will be moving up and down once for every inch of yarn. At the sunny beginning of a project, you gladly commit to flapping your foot for whatever it takes to get the yarn. However, if you have an alternative that will give you two or three times the length of yarn in the same amount of time, and with the same effort... well, think about it. Choose the tool that gives you a reasonable production rate. Sometimes that tool is not a treadled wheel. More about that later.

Wheel Maintenance

All wheels benefit from good maintenance. Unless your wheel manufacturer instructs differently, oil everything that moves. To make fine yarn, you have to treadle briskly. Your wheel runs on lubrication.

On the mother-of-all, there are four oiling points:
- Front flyer bearing
- Back flyer bearing
- Front bobbin bearing
- Back bobbin bearing

On the wheel posts, there are often three oiling points:
- Front-wheel post bearing
- Back-wheel post bearing
- Footman-to-crank bearing

On the treadle, there are often two oiling points:
- The treadle bearing on each end of the treadle at the legs

It's always a good idea to remove the bobbin from time to time and wipe the flyer shaft with a clean rag to remove old oil and fibers that accumulate there. Also check the crank and drive wheel bearings for dirt and fiber. Clean often and re-oil the flyer/bobbin area every 20 to 30 minutes of high-speed spinning. The wheel posts and crank need oil about once a day; the treadle, once a week.

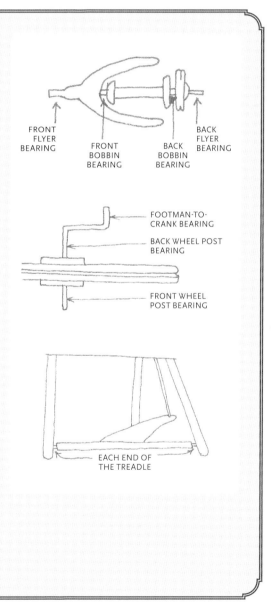

FRONT FLYER BEARING
FRONT BOBBIN BEARING
BACK BOBBIN BEARING
BACK FLYER BEARING

FOOTMAN-TO-CRANK BEARING
BACK WHEEL POST BEARING
FRONT WHEEL POST BEARING

EACH END OF THE TREADLE

Using the Flyer/Bobbin Wheel

Thread the leader out through the orifice and, with a few treads, join on the fiber. Your leader can be wool or cotton two-ply commercial yarn. Although it's easiest to join the fiber onto a cotton yarn, wool can work.

Your two hands are going to do two separate and significant jobs. Your lead hand (the one closest to the flyer) will do the big job of keeping the wheel from sucking in the yarn, yet permitting the right amount of twist past it as you draft, extend, and finish the yarn. The fiber hand acts as a distaff, gently supporting the fiber until it's time to work in tandem with the lead hand to draft out the slubs and wind on.

So here goes… treadle slowly. Begin to draft back with the fiber hand, with the lead hand remaining stationary about 12" (30.5 cm) away from the orifice.

When you get about 10" (25.5 cm) of fiber drawn out into a soft, slubby "string," stop treadling. This 10" (25.5 cm) length should have soft, twisted thin spots separated by areas with no twist at all. Now your fiber hand can move forward as you use your thumb and forefinger to pinch the forming yarn below the drafting zone. (Doing so keeps the twist out of the fiber until the next bit of yarn is drafted.) Begin treadling slowly. Again, your lead hand will keep the wheel from taking the yarn while permitting more twist to enter the forming yarn. At the same time, begin to move your fiber hand slowly away from the wheel to extend the yarn.

Draft the yarn between your hands by pulling on the fiber-hand end. As the slubs are converted to smooth yarn, increase your treadling rate a bit. Don't let go of the yarn with the lead hand until the yarn is strong. While treadling, you can test the strength of the yarn by pulling

DRAFTING ON THE FLYER/BOBBIN WHEEL

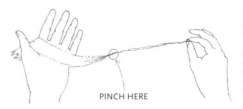

PINCH HERE

Draft back with your fiber hand.

Move your fiber hand forward and pinch the forming yarn below the drafting zone.

Move your hands apart to extend the yarn.

---

it between your hands, letting some twist through, and gently increasing the pull until the yarn is strong. When you feel firm yarn, let go with your lead hand and gradually let the wheel take the yarn onto the bobbin.

At the beginning of the next draw, pull back quickly. There will be a slub caused by the twist in the yarn you just made. The yarn that's not wound onto the bobbin will have a lot of twist that swiftly travels into the soft yarn you're now making. When you draft out fiber, the twist will transfer to that newly drafted

MAKING JOINS

Untwist a slub until the fibers run parallel, then pull the yarn apart.

Lay the "brush" end of the yarn on the end of the fiber.

Gently pull back on the fiber to permit twist to travel up the yarn and into the drafting area.

fiber. Keep your lead hand at the interface between the strong yarn and the forming yarn. Using your lead hand as a gate, open and shut it to allow twist through at intervals. Treadle slowly so you don't put too much twist into the yarn ahead of your lead hand.

Making Joins

This is a good time to discuss joins and how to make them. When yarn breaks or drifts apart, it often jumps onto the bobbin. That brief moment of freedom allows the tail of the yarn to untwist, resulting in several inches of yarn that's no longer sound—it's no longer a yarn.

Carefully work back to strong yarn, unwinding some yarn off the bobbin by hand if necessary. When you come to strong yarn, don't let go of it until you have worked it across the hooks and threaded it through the orifice. Once the yarn is threaded through the orifice, keep a good hold on the end while you find a thick spot in it. Untwist that thick spot until you see the fibers running parallel. Pull the yarn apart.

This process gives you a yarn to join onto, a yarn with two important qualities: plenty of twist ahead of the join and a soft, brushlike end. With about 12" (30.5 cm) of yarn out of the orifice, lay the "brush" end of the joining yarn on the end of your fiber. If there's a remnant of a yarn on the end of the fiber, pull that remnant off and discard it so there's a soft brushy end on that, too.

Resist the impulse to pat the yarn into the fiber. Just lay it in contact with the fiber mass. Gently pull back on the fiber to permit the twist to travel up the yarn and into the drafting area. With practice, this will result in a drafted join upon which you can depend!

When your yarn breaks, take it as an opportunity to practice joining. The more times you do it, the better the join and the faster you become.[4]

---

4 This join works on not only cotton but all kinds of fibers: wools, hairs, silks, and bast fiber in sliver form. Bast fibers in "line" fiber preparation do not work unless you have really long arms.

Frequently Asked Questions

Q. *How does your lead hand manage to hold onto the yarn and still let twist through?*

A. There are a number of ways you can let twist past your fingers without letting go completely.

Option 1: You can roll the yarn in the twist direction. Doing so permits a small amount of twist through, which is useful at the beginning of the draft.

Option 2: You can decrease how tightly you squeeze the yarn, which can let twist slip through. But to work, the twisted yarn ahead of your lead hand needs to be fairly firmly twisted.

Option 3: You can use your thumb and index finger to pinch the yarn, palm down, and use your ring finger and pinky finger to gently squeeze the yarn as well.

First, open your pinky/ring fingers to allow twist to travel into the yarn that spans your palm—the twist will stop where your index/thumb fingers are squeezed shut. Then, close your pinky/ring fingers and open your index/thumb fingers to release that twist behind your lead hand. Close your index/thumb fingers. Open the finger pair closest to the wheel, then close it and open the finger pair farthest from the wheel, releasing twist between your hands. It's sort of like the "itsy bitsy spider" crawling along the yarn, but it works. This method takes some practice but it does keep the wheel from winding on, and, when you're familiar with how it goes, you can quickly release a fair quantity of twist.

WAYS TO HOLD THE YARN AND LET TWIST PASS THROUGH YOUR FINGERS

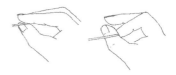

At the beginning of a draft, roll the yarn in the twist direction to allow a small amount of twist through.

Alternate using your thumb and index finger to pinch the yarn, then using your ring and pinky fingers to squeeze the yarn.

Retard the twist by bending the yarn.

Option 4: You can use deflection to retard twist almost as certainly as pinching it off. As the yarn comes out from the orifice, make it bend around one of your lead hands fingers.

If you nearly straighten the yarn, more twist gets past your lead hand. If you make a sharp bend, no twist will travel behind your lead hand. This is good technique for hands that tire quickly.

WAYS TO ENSURE THERE'S ENOUGH TWIST

Pull a section between your hands.

Let go of your lead hand, then

permit the yarn to wind on slowly.

For a final check, strip out a length of yarn that's already on the bobbin and let it fold back on itself.

Q. *How do I know if I have enough twist?*

A. The first test is what you do before you let the yarn wind on the bobbin. Pull that section of yarn between your hands before you let go of the lead hand and permit the yarn to wind on. This will add twist the whole time it travels in and will ensure that the yarn is sound before it's wound onto the bobbin.

The second test is to strip out a length of yarn that's already on the bobbin and let it fold back on itself. The resulting two-ply yarn should look like beads on a string—the humps in the ply standing "shoulder to shoulder" with each other. If your yarn looks like this, your singles will make good warp yarn and the plies will make durable, soft knitting yarn.

Q. *My yarn falls apart when I try to unwind it off the bobbin. What am I doing wrong?*

A. First, don't let go of the yarn. If it has slipped out of your hands and is wound on the bobbin, lift the end off the bobbin and check the yarn for sufficient twist. If the yarn has drawn into the bobbin on its own, both the action of the whirling flyer and cotton's nature, which causes it to lose twist when unsupported, will conspire to make 12" to 24" (30.5 to 61 cm) of insubstantial yarn (that is, without enough twist to be yarn anymore). If you have just such a yarn, break off the punk yarn at a slub, then thread the good yarn over the hooks and through the orifice without letting go of the yarn. Join the fiber, and you're back to spinning. The point is: don't let go of the yarn except when you stop spinning and wind it onto the bobbin.

If you find that more than 12" to 24" (30.5 to 61 cm) of yarn doesn't have enough twist, then you have a larger problem. You're letting the yarn wind on before it has enough twist to make it yarn. Hold onto it while treadling and let the wheel take it slowly. Be aware of your drafting style and change it, if necessary, so that you get enough twist to finish the yarn as it winds on. In this case, the term "finish" means the yarn has reached the desired twist at the point where it winds onto the bobbin. Keep in mind that this is an ideal, but not a real, situation. The bobbin core is constantly changing its circumference and capacity to wind on a given length of yarn. Cross-reeling your yarn will help to equalize the twist (see page 116).

Using Handspindles

So far, you've seen that it's possible to spin cotton on the more familiar flyer/bobbin wheel. However, there are tools with roots more firmly planted in history and prehistory that make spinning cotton vastly simpler. With practice, these tools do the job with great efficiency and speed.

The cotton handspindle has been used for centuries in many parts of the world, from South America to Central Asia, and from Africa to India. Spindles that are useful cotton tools fall into three main types: tip-supported, mid-whorl, and suspended high-whorl.

Tip-Supported Spindles

Tip-supported spindles are usually placed in a smooth bowl when used. The sharp point on the bottom of the spindle shaft spins in the smooth bowl with little friction. The pointed tip permits the spindle to turn briskly and the weight of the whorl lets it continue rotating for some time.

Tip-supported spindles are found in a variety of materials and forms. One common type has a slender shaft with a ceramic, wood, bone, or glass bead for a whorl. This type is called a bead-whorl spindle for obvious reasons. A very efficient tip-supported spindle is the tahkli—an all-metal spindle with a disk low on the shaft and a sharp point at both ends. One end is flattened and notched. A tip-sup-ported spindle can also be whorl-less, as in the Russian-style spindle. Russian spindles are one piece with a shaft tapered at each end and a carved recess in the middle for winding on the yarn.

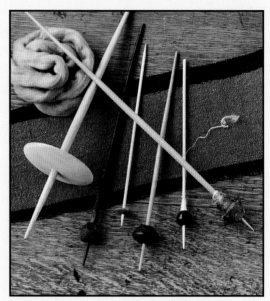

Cotton handspindles have been used for centuries.

Spindles with sharp points are usually placed in a smooth bowl when used. Left to right: **tahkli**, **Peruvian**, **Nigerian**, **beadwhorl**, and **Russian**.

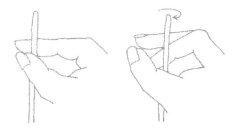

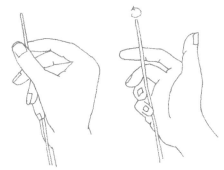

To "snap" the spindle, swipe your middle or index finger along your thumb as if you were snapping your fingers.

Flicking is the same as snapping, but in the opposite direction.

Place the sharp tip of the spindle in a bowl and practice snapping and flicking to determine which is easiest for you.

Tip-supported spindles are spun with a snapping or flicking motion of your thumb and forefinger. With the exception of the tahkli, your index or middle finger and thumb are placed right up near or at the top of the pointy shaft. To "snap" the spindle, swipe your middle or index finger along your thumb and toward the palm of your hand. This "snapping" motion is similar to snapping your fingers. Because the tahkli has a shaped tip that carries the yarn, you'll want to snap it with your fingers below the tip.

Flicking is the same movement as snapping, but in the opposite direction. The index or middle finger starts down on the pad of the thumb and pushes the spindle tip away from the center of the palm.

Put the sharp tip of your spindle in the bowl and alternate snapping and flicking until you get a sense for which direction your hand wants to go. It really doesn't matter which direction you choose, so pick the one that seems natural to you.

To practice spinning with a tip-supported spindle, get some ready-to-spin fiber and join it to a leader (sewing thread makes a great leader for small spindles). You'll see a tahkli spindle in the photos of this technique.

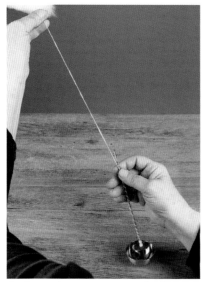

Draft out about 10" (25.5 cm) of soft, barely spun yarn.

Pinch off the twist well below the drafting zone.

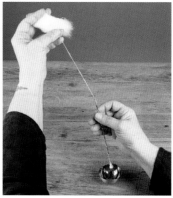

Turn the spindle more briskly while extending the unformed yarn.

Add twist until the yarn is strong and won't draft further.

Begin by turning your spindle, slowly at first. Use the same procedure as for spinning on a wheel to draft out a soft, barely spun yarn, about 10" (25.5 cm) long, then pinch off the twist on the soft yarn, well below the drafting zone.

Begin to turn the spindle more briskly while extending the unformed, not completely spun "yarn." Continue extending it while putting in twist until it won't draft further.

Turn the spindle in the opposite direction to clear the tip of the spindle.

Holding the yarn at right angles to the spindle, wind it on in the same direction as you spun the yarn, leaving about 5" (12.5 cm) of yarn coming off the tip of the spindle. Don't let go of the end of the yarn, or you'll lose twist.

USING A TIP-SUPPORTED SPINDLE

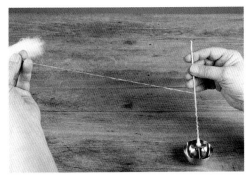

Turn the spindle in the opposite direction to clear the shaft.

Hold the yarn perpendicular to the spindle and wind the yarn on in the same direction as it was spun.

Keep your fingers close to the spindle tip to prevent it from falling over.

When you begin your next draw, draft a small amount (maybe 1" to 2" [2.5 to 5 cm]) before you turn the spindle. Doing so uses up some of the twist in the yarn that might tend to run up into the fiber—remember, too much twist can make drafting difficult to impossible. This small initial draft also takes care of the slub that can form at the beginning of your draft.

The key to using a tip-supported spindle is that you never let go of the spindle. Your fingers are always either putting in twist or letting the spindle coast (the traditional term is "cast") while it's surrounded by your thumb and index or middle finger. If you do let go, the spindle will tip and fall over sideways, the yarn might break, and you'll lose your spinning rhythm. (This isn't a good thing.)

Mid-Whorl Spindles

The mid-whorl spindle is a hand-supported spindle. You hold it in your hand while drafting the yarn, putting in twist, and winding on. The spindle never leaves your hand. Types of mid-whorl spindles include the akha or Thai-style, Salish, and Pueblo spindles. A mid-whorl spindle shorter than 18" (45.5 cm) with a thin disk whorl of 3" (7.5 cm) or less can efficiently spin a fine cotton yarn.

Spinning on a mid-whorl spindle is fairly straightforward. First, get used to the spindle's heft and balance by rotating it first in one direction and then the other until you have a sense of which direction is best for you. Practice rotating the spindle until you can keep the tip steady—it shouldn't waver, scribe a circle, or jerk about.

The akha is a mid-whorl spindle.

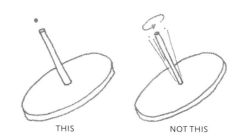

THIS   NOT THIS

The spindle tip should not waver as it turns.

To begin, wind the leader up the spindle shaft and lay it on top of the fiber supply. Rotate the spindle a couple of times. Then, without turning the spindle, gently pull on the leader to transfer the twist into the fiber supply and drafting zone. You should see the end of the leader yarn begin to entwine the loose fibers.

While rotating the spindle, gently pull the fiber into the drafting zone and into a softly spun yarn. When you have about 10" (25.5 cm) of soft yarn, pinch off the twist on the yarn below the drafting zone with your thumb and forefinger to keep twist out of the unspun fiber.

Add twist and pull between your hands to extend the yarn and draft out the slubs. Continue to add twist and pull the yarn thinner until it stops drifting. A fine yarn involves

a fair amount of spindle twiddling. Don't worry about the yarn falling over the spindle tip; it's supposed to do that.

Add more twist, then rotate the spindle in the opposite direction to clear the spindle tip.

Twisting your yarn in the same direction as you spun it, wind your yarn onto the spindle shaft. Leave about 10" (25.5 cm) of yarn for your next draft. Depending on the balance of the spindle, the length of the shaft below the whorl and your personal preference, you can wind the yarn above the whorl, below the whorl, or both.

Before you begin to rotate the spindle at the beginning of the next draw, draft out a few inches of soft yarn. Doing so will use up some of the twist from the strong yarn and let you begin drafting from the fiber mass more easily.

SPINNING ON A MID-WHORL SPINDLE

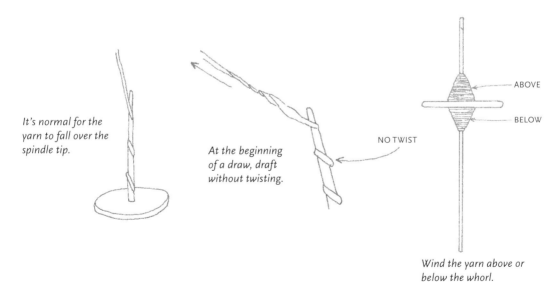

It's normal for the yarn to fall over the spindle tip.

At the beginning of a draw, draft without twisting.

NO TWIST

ABOVE

BELOW

Wind the yarn above or below the whorl.

There's an advanced technique you can use to put in twist more rapidly on a mid-whorl spindle (such as an akha). When you have a good length of yarn drafted and are ready to put in the final twist to make it strong, drop the fiber side spindle tip to rest it on the yarn. Hold the spindle not against your palm as before, but with your fingers clustered at the far tip. Add twist until the yarn can take the weight of the spindle without drifting apart, and then put in the final twist with a few brisk flicks. The spindle will be cantilevered off one hand, with one tip resting on the yarn. In this position, the spindle is free to whirl at greater speed.

The akha isn't known as a fast spindle, but it's sturdy, easy to pack along, and lets you work in limited space. For those reasons, it's a welcome addition to any spinner's kit.

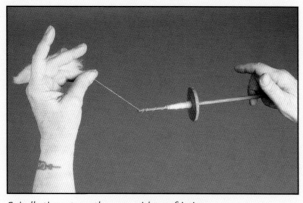

Spindle tip rests on the yarn without friction.

About my tattoo—it's a skein of yarn flanked by a spindle at each end. I've worn it since 1982.

Suspended High-Whorl Spindles

Suspended spindles hang from the yarn they're making. For spinning a fine cotton yarn, you'll be restricted to very lightweight versions. But lightweight spindles often have a short "cast" or duration of spin. One way to compensate for this is to run it down or up your thigh using the palm of your hand before releasing it to get some momentum going. At high speeds, a well-balanced and proportioned high-whorl spindle has decent stability.[5]

Lightweight versions of this type of spindle can produce some quite fine yarns. If your goal is to spin high-twist yarns, however, this spindle does have limitations. The problem is with consistency. A lightweight spindle gains weight as you wind your yarn onto it. The yarn you spin must become thicker to support the heavier spindle as more and more yarn is wound onto the shaft. And here's the problem: thicker yarns take less twist to become rigid enough to stall the spindle. With the added weight, the spindle can continue to deliver good high twist. However, you'll have to stop eventually because the "full spindle yarn" becomes a different size and has different twist from what you started with.

Before you practice spinning cotton on a suspended high-whorl spindle, let's talk a bit about what you're going to do. Your lead hand (the one running the spindle) does the big job. It keeps the spindle going while producing just

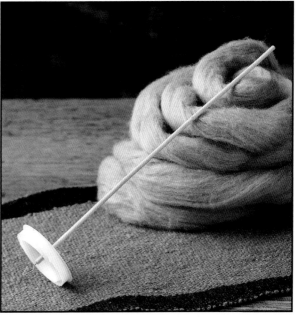

Only very lightweight suspended spindles with high-whorls can be used to spin fine cotton yarn. Spindle shown courtesy of Jim Conti.

the right amount of twist between your hands. The fiber hand does its best to gently support the fiber and not compress or disarrange it until it's time to pinch off the twist and draft the slubs. Drafting the fiber is a deliberate act between your hands. The yarn formed in the drafting zone isn't strong enough to support the spindle, so the lead hand will have to do the drafting rather than letting the weight of the spindle do it. Let's try it.

---

5 At high speeds, spindles can perform like gyroscopes, defying gravity with the spindle shaft nearly parallel to the floor. A low-whorl spindle can readily disconnect from the yarn at the top of the spindle shaft during such a maneuver. Depending on hook profile, high-whorl spindles can maintain better contact with the yarn.

To begin, wind a threadlike leader from the spindle shaft below the whorl, then up around the hook. Put a little twist into the leader and join onto your fiber supply.

Give the spindle a little twist and begin to draft a soft yarn between your hands. Draft and slowly twist until you have about 10" (25.5 cm) of soft yarn.

Pinch off the twist just below the drafting zone.

Add more twist and draft out the yarn between your hands, adding twist until it's as fine and strong as you want it to be.

Note: You may find that deflecting the yarn works better than rolling or pinching (see page 36) to keep the twist under control as you draft. To use the technique, let the intersection of firm yarn and forming yarn lie across your lead hand thumb, palm down. Rest your index finger or middle finger on top of the yarn lightly. You're holding the forming yarn horizontal while the spindle hangs down from this point.

If you change the angle of the yarn in this position, you'll be able to let more or less twist go through your thumb and fingers. Straight-line, vertical yarn permits the most twist through the "gate" made by your thumb and fingers. A right-angle bend in the yarn makes the twist less vigorous, because the gate is "closed." To give the spindle another flick, move your fiber hand to the intersection of forming and firm yarn, and pinch there.

You should now have firm yarn between your hands, and you'll be able to add twist with your palm. While the spindle is rapidly turning, move your lead hand to that gate point and let your fiber hand open and resume its job of supporting the fiber and pinching off the twist ahead of the drafting zone.

When the yarn is strong enough to support the weight of the spindle, give the spindle a final few flicks to finish off the yarn. Check the yarn to make sure it's strong and well spun.

Unhook the yarn from the spindle top and wind on yarn beneath the whorl, leaving 8" to 10" (20.5 to 25.5 cm) of yarn off the hook before you begin to draft another length of soft yarn.

You won't have much time while spinning to gaze at the clouds and wonder what's for lunch. This type of spindle keeps your hands busy and your attention riveted. Mastering cotton spinning on a spindle demands practice and diligence. After you become adept at spinning with one spindle, each new spindle you try is easier, much like learning a new language. The advantage to becoming proficient on a spindle is that you can tuck it in a purse, backpack, or jacket pocket and put those odd moments to good use—waiting for the kettle to boil, standing in line, traveling, talking to friends on the phone. It's remarkable how much yarn can accrue in "stolen moments." In fact, hand skills are more quickly mastered if you practice for many short sessions rather than one long one.

USING A SUSPENDED HIGH-WHORL SPINDLE

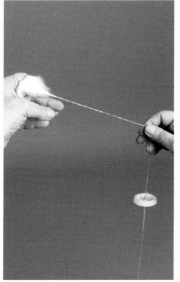

Give the spindle a little twist and draft a soft yarn between your hands.

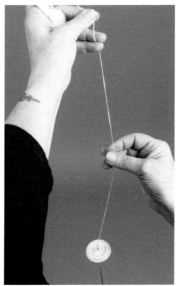

Finish off the yarn.

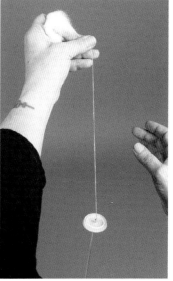

Pinch off the twist below the drafting zone; draft yarn between your hands.

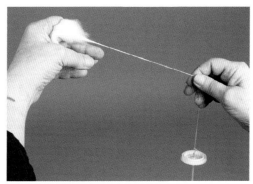

Deflect the yarn to control the twist.

Using the Charkha

Charkhas were developed in those parts of the world where cotton originated: India, China, and Persia. They're basically spindles driven by a hand-operated drive wheel. The ratio between the circumference of the spindle and the circumference of the drive wheel is large, which means this device can supply enormous amounts of twist, with no take-up. Thus, charkhas have the perfect combination of characteristics for spinning cotton. Charkhas have many forms, but can be classed into two major categories: simple and accelerated.

The Simple Charkha

The simple charkha has one drive wheel and a spindle, held together in a frame. The wheel is typically mounted on a single or pair of posts set into a base. The wheel can be solid or composed of slats or a web of strings. Sometimes, there's a hand crank. Whether the wheel is elegant or crude, it functions the same way. Turn the wheel, and the spindle goes around and makes yarn. Variations on this wheel appear across India, Asia, Turkey, and Iran. Its European/North American cousin is the great wheel.

Because a charkha can go very fast, it needs lubrication at regular intervals. Most flat bearings do well with a little oil, frequently applied. Oil everything that moves. Check with the manufacturer for lubricant suggestions, locations, and schedules.

A simple charkha needs few adjustments. The first is drive-cord tension. Move the spindle mother-of-all back and forth while turning the wheel. You'll find a point that will permit good engagement with the drive wheel. You don't normally need a lot of tension on the drive cord for this engagement—just enough for the spindle to turn readily without slipping when you turn the drive wheel.

ADJUSTMENTS FOR THE SIMPLE CHARKHA

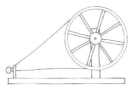

The simple charkha has one drive wheel and a spindle held in a frame.

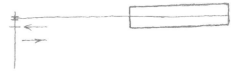

To adjust the drive cord tension, move the spindle mother-of-all back and forth until the spindle turns readily without slipping.

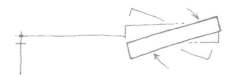

Rotate the wheel post until the drive wheel is perpendicular to the spindle.

Slightly rotate the mother-of-all to adjust the "float" of the spindle whorl between the two bearings.

If your charkha has a single post supporting the drive wheel, you have another alignment to consider to keep the drive cord on the wheel. The drive cord "tracks" or stays on the drive wheel when the axle of the drive wheel is at a right angle to the spindle. You can rotate the wheel post to make this adjustment.

SPINNING ON A SIMPLE CHARKHA

Turn the wheel slowly as you draft about 20" (51 cm) of soft slubby yarn.

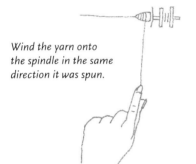

Use your fiber hand to pinch the twist below the drafting zone.

Extend the soft yarn until the slubs are gone.

Wind the yarn onto the spindle in the same direction it was spun.

The other adjustment is for the "float" of the spindle whorl between the two bearings. Some charkhas have little to no adjustment of float. The mother-of-all on these machines is rigid and can't be rotated to permit less thrust on the front bearing. If your wheel's mother-of-all can be realigned, slightly rotate it so that the spindle whorl drifts to the back bearing while you turn the wheel with the drive cord in place. As you draft your yarn, the spindle whorl will migrate to the front bearing with less tendency to jam up against it.

Spinning on the Simple Charkha

On a simple charkha, the spinning technique is similar to that on a supported spindle, except that it happens much faster.

To begin, lay your leader—sewing or quilting thread will do—on the fiber supply and, without drafting, give the drive wheel a turn or two.

Stop turning the wheel. Gently pull the fiber supply back from the wheel a bit. Doing so transfers the twist to the fiber, joining the fiber onto the leader. If it doesn't do it the first time, add more twist and pull back again. Avoid over-handling the fiber at this point. Just lay the leader yarn on the fiber and pull a bit. Watch that twist transfer to the cotton in the fiber mass.

Turn the wheel slowly while you draft, rather quickly, about 20" (51 cm) of soft, slubby yarn.

With your fiber hand, pinch the yarn below the drafting zone.

Begin to simultaneously pull on the soft yarn and slowly rotate the wheel. Twist should begin to accumulate in the thin spots of the yarn. Continue turning the wheel slowly and drafting slowly until you've drafted all the slubs into much thinner yarn with an overall greater length. (This process may take several trials until the motion becomes familiar. That's okay. You're learning to see two things at once: where the twist is, and how much is there.)

Add more twist to the yarn—enough to make it strong and sound.

Turn the wheel the other direction to clear the spindle tip.

Wind yarn onto the spindle, going the same direction in which you spun the yarn.

The Accelerated Charkha

An accelerated charkha came into my life after I'd been spinning cotton on an Ashford wheel or a tahkli for several years. I sat down to try it at 10:00 p.m., saying to myself, "I'll just see what it can do." I entered some time warp, because it was 3:30 a.m. when I tried to stand, and found myself stumbling around the room, amazed and in a new world.

The accelerated charkha has two wheels. One large wheel that drives a smaller wheel, which drives the spindle. It's two to three times faster than the simple charkha. Simple charkhas have wheel ratios ranging from about 10-to-1 (or 10 rotations on the spindle to 1 turn of the wheel) to 40-to-1 for a modest-sized drive wheel. The accelerated charkha wheel ratios, in contrast, are in the 80-to-1 to 120-to-1 range. That's fast!

Although accelerated wheels come in many sizes and variations, they share similar mechanical principles and other characteristics. Primarily, they're fine yarn spinners. By fine yarn, I mean, finer than 8,000 yards per pound (14,630 meters per kilogram)—imagine a singles yarn the size of #60 Cordonnet crochet cotton. If you try to spin too coarse a yarn on this device, you'll run into problems.

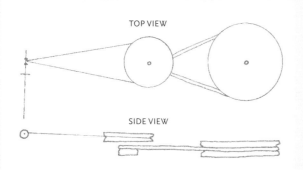

The accelerated charkha has two wheels.

The spindle stalls and the yarn won't wind on. Instead of a smooth cylinder, the yarn looks like twisted rags. It all goes downhill fast.

Spinning on the Accelerated Charkha

Before you start to spin on an accelerated charkha, check the wheel's lubrication needs with its manufacturer. These tools perform at high speeds, and what might seem to be minor friction can stall the spindle or make it perform erratically. At the least, wipe the bearings down and clean off all the fluff and goo.

Spinning on an accelerated charkha is similar to spinning on the simple charkha, only much faster.

To begin, join onto a sewing thread leader with a few turns of the smaller wheel.

Pull back on the fiber supply, transferring the twist to the drafting zone.

Holding the fiber with a light touch (no squashing!), put in a bit more twist using the small wheel and begin to draft back, releasing about 10" (25.5 cm) of soft, barely spun, somewhat slubby yarn.

Pinch off below the drafting zone so the twist won't bury itself in the fiber supply.

Shift over to the larger wheel and draft out the soft yarn while rotating the larger wheel to add twist and extend slubs. Note that if it won't draft, it's because you've already put in too much twist. Take it slowly until you become accustomed to the speed at which the accelerated wheel puts in twist.

When you have a length of solid yarn, turn the smaller wheel in the opposite direction to clear the spindle tip.

Use the smaller wheel to wind your finished yarn onto the base of the spindle near the cop disk (the whorl on the spindle blade), turning in the same direction as you spun the yarn.

SPINNING ON AN ACCELERATED CHARKHA

Use the small wheel to draft back, releasing about 10" (25.5 cm) of soft slubby yarn.

Pinch off below the drafting zone.

Use the large wheel to add twist and extend slubs.

Turn the small wheel in the opposite direction to clear the spindle tip.

Use the smaller wheel to wind the yarn onto the base of the spindle.

The whorl keeps fiber out of the spindle bearings and lets you build a conical-shaped yarn package (see Chapter 4 for more on yarn handling).

Bette Hochberg once told me that the best teacher for spinning cotton was a pound (.45 kg) of it. After you've spun the pound of cotton, you'll have a pretty good idea of what it takes to manage the fiber, the tools, and the twist. Bette delivered this lesson while wearing a fabulous dress made entirely out of hand-spun, handwoven brown cotton. Wow!

Frequently Asked Questions

Q. *My yarn is too fat. How do I make it smaller?*

A. Draft back more quickly when you're making the soft beginning yarn. Doing so lets you extend the yarn into finer yarn as you finish off the twist.

Q. *I can't get the yarn to wind on. I turn the wheel, but nothing happens.*

A. You're not letting the yarn wind on. You can easily stall the spindle by pulling back on it even a little bit. Let up a bit on the yarn as you wind on. You may be spinning too large a yarn as well. Draft back more quickly and extend your soft yarn out farther.

Q. *The spindle makes a funny noise—like a vibration—when I turn the wheel fast.*

A. The Indians call that the charkha's "purr." It's most likely normal, but if your wheel can be lubricated, do so to see if that reduces the sound.

Q. *The leader is gone from the wheel. Do I really need one?*

A. Not really. Having a leader is easier for beginners, but old hands just wipe a bit of oil on the spindle blade and, with the fiber at a right angle to the spindle, turn the wheel to make the blade contact a few of the longer fibers. The oil makes the fibers stick to the blade. An inch (2.5 cm) or so from the end of the spindle, let the longer fibers layer themselves onto the blade until they have firmly attached themselves. Then move the fiber mass to a point just off the end of the spindle and add twist while you draft a leader of about 10" (25.5 cm). Extend and add enough twist to the yarn to make it firm. Carefully slide that layered sheath of fibers down the blade to the disk, then wind on the yarn.

Q. *The yarn got away from me. Now I can't find the end of the yarn. What do I do?*

A. This is a sad time. You can look for the end and maybe you'll be able to find it. My answer is to pull or cut the yarn off the spindle and start over, making sure that this time your yarn has plenty of twist. Soft yarns are easily fouled and imbedded; firm yarns, not so much.

STARTING WITHOUT A LEADER

Hold the fiber perpendicular to the spindle and turn the wheel to catch a few fibers.

Move the fiber mass to the spindle tip.

Add twist while you draft about 10" (25.5 cm) of fiber.

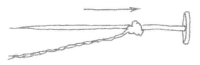

Slide the yarn down the spindle shaft.

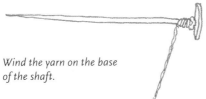

Wind the yarn on the base of the shaft.

CHAPTER TWO:

Flax

Sometimes I ask myself, "Why do I bother with flax?" Getting the fiber ready to spin requires so many steps. Then, when it's spun, the yarn is like wire: stiff and willful. But the fact is, I love the stuff. I love the messy, time-consuming job of turning stiff stems into pliable, silky fibers. I love the lustrous, elegant yarns and the fabrics made from them.

Plant materials such as flax are transformed during the making. If you look only at the original material or the finished cloth, you miss most of the fun—all the amazing things that happen in between! This is not to say that you have to start with planting seeds to be a flax spinner. There are plenty of flax preparations on the market, just waiting to be spun. But let's take it from the beginning.

Flax Species

FLAX (*LINUM USITATISSIMUM*) is a bast fiber, along with hemp and ramie. The spinnable bast fibers reside in the long stems, between the outer "skin" or cuticle and the pith core. In the field and as it's prepared for spinning, it is called flax. Once spun, it becomes "linen."

Bast fibers have roots stretching back for thousands of years. In many cultures worldwide, they're archetypal, ancient, crowned with special status. They grace the modern home, play their part in celebrating seasons and traditions, and create a tangible link to the past. They have commanded regal performances, clothed the humble who could afford little else, and bound Pharaoh for the afterlife. They're the very stuff of history.

Textile-quality bast fibers are present in a multitude of plants. The most familiar are flax, hemp, and ramie. But besides these there are hops, jute, stinging nettle, milkweed, and several tree species—and more. *Matthews' Textile Fibers*, published in 1913, lists nine major and nineteen minor bast fibers. The focus in this chapter is on flax; Chapter 3 will cover hemp.

Ramie ribbon.

Assorted bast fibers.

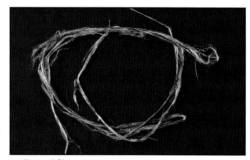

Milkweed fibers.

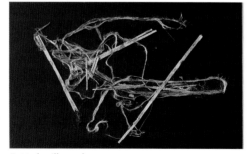

Retted milkweed

The bast fibers share many desirable qualities. As fine singles, they're worthy candidates for heirloom garments and linens.[6] Plied into larger yarns, they excel in heavy-traffic areas, such as door mats, rug warps, or finer yarns for upholstery and draperies. Bast fibers also have a venerable history as rope, cordage, and canvas. They're strong, resistant to wear and tear, and not damaged by exposure to sunlight.

Depending on how they've been processed and spun, bast fibers can have considerable luster. A trick of light occurs in cloth woven with a single color. This gleaming fabric combines finely divided, broken surfaces with smooth ones. The areas reflect light differently. This subtle pattern appears in an elegant weave known as damask.

Flax and hemp make delightful summer wear because they're absorbent, smooth, and cool. The hollow cellular structure wicks away moisture and heat. Bast fibers are champions in the realm of laundry, too. None of the laundering conditions (caustic pH, boiling water, agitation) damage the bast fibers. In fact, they're stronger when wet. Flax and hemp dry quickly, too.

However, nestled among these positive attributes lurk real challenges for the unwary spinner. Flax and hemp yarns, even when finely spun, are stiff, wiry, rigid, and inelastic. These yarns certainly do not behave in hand-wound balls—much less the trickier center-pull balls. They require special treatment when being wound on a bobbin or spindle. Further, the strength of flax and hemp becomes a negative if you try to break them with your hands—you can't.

6 Linen was a generic term for usage, as in "household" linens: sheets, towels, tablecloths, napkins. Historically, "linen" could be made from nettle, hops, flax, hemp, or even cotton.

This lace handkerchief from the Amos family was made with fine linen.

Detail of handkerchief.

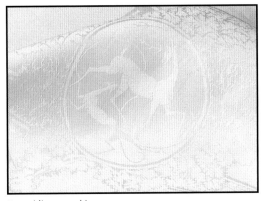

Borzoi linen napkin.

Flax Fiber Characteristics

THE SOURCE FOR BAST FIBERS, including flax, lies within the stem of the plant. Fibrous structures run the length of the stem, transporting food to and from the leaves and roots and giving the stem flexibility and strength. Bast fibers are the phloem, thick-walled tubes that grow just beneath the bark. In cross-section you can see next to the plant "skin" a ring of phloem mingled with smaller structures surrounding the woody core. The phloem is cemented in place by water-soluble gums and pectin.

A remarkable thing about bast fibers is their considerable length: 2 to 3 feet (61 to 91.5 cm) long or more, depending upon species and growing conditions. Flax is typically 24" to 40" (61 to 101.5 cm) tall in the field; hemp can reach 8 feet (2.4 meters) or more.

Flax shares many of the mixed-bag qualities of other bast fibers: it's inelastic, cool to the touch, and abrasion-resistant. It's a strong fiber (even stronger when wet), and quick drying. It wrinkles easily and those wrinkles won't hang out. It's resistant to caustics such as lye, but acids, even mild ones, damage or destroy it. Chemical bleaches weaken it, but you can boil it to make it sanitary and to whiten it. Mildews and molds destroy the fiber.

Unique to flax among the bast fibers, however, are its great strength (it's the strongest natural fiber), its absorbency (it's the most absorbent of all natural fibers), and its resistance to damage from ultraviolet light. Sunlight only makes it whiter, so it's a wonderful material for curtains in a sunny window. Spun from strick (more about that later), linen yarn is lustrous and naturally shiny.

Linen yarns are more flexible when wet than dry. A bit of water, judiciously applied, will aid both the spinner and weaver. The lack of it produces another effect on linens. Flax is vulnerable in very low humidity (say, in the single digits). In this situation, it breaks instead of bending—a forgotten, lengthy tumble in a hot dryer will do serious injury to your linens.

Flax fiber comes in many colors. It can be soft dove gray, dark pewter, creamy beige, or deep manila. Fiber flax is colored because of the processing the fiber has undergone, the minerals in the soil, the location where it grew, and genetics. Be aware that these lovely, quiet earth tones are not permanent, though.

Flax is about 78 percent cellulose. By nature, pure cellulose is white. Besides cellulose, the remaining fiber components are mostly waxes, pectin, and gums. Being water soluble, they will wash out. This causes three changes in your yarn. It turns white; the once wiry and stiff yarn transforms into a lean, dense one; and it gets finer by about 25 percent. (This is a serious loss, as it affects the set of a woven cloth or the gauge of a knitted one.) Before the pectin, waxes, and gums are removed, however, they are very useful in the spinning process. But we get ahead of ourselves. Let's take a look at the process of how flax grows before we go into harvest and fiber preparation.

Flax comes in a variety of natural shades.

Flax spinning fibers are found in the stem portion of the plant just beneath the plant's "skin" or cuticle. If you were to cut across the stem, you would see a peripheral layer of skin cells and next, bundles of large, thick-walled tubular structures called phloem, which carry nutrients between the leaves and the roots.

The phloem is made up of single cells, or "ultimates"—long (1" [2.5 cm] or longer) cells that are pointed at each end. These cells are glued together with pectin. In cross-section, the phloem tube is five- or six-sided with "nodes" or nobs (swollen bumps like the joints on bamboo or cane) where the ultimates overlap one another.[7]

7 One way to distinguish cotton from flax fiber is to observe them under magnification. Cotton is seen as twisted ribbons, whereas flax has nodes.

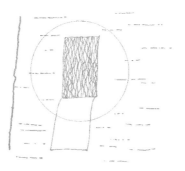

Bast fibers lie beneath the bark.

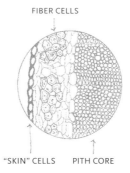

FIBER CELLS
"SKIN" CELLS   PITH CORE

Flax spinning fibers are found in the stem portion of the plant just beneath the skin or cuticle.

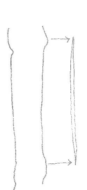

Ultimates are long single cells that are pointed at each end.

Nodes are formed where ultimates overlap.

Growing Flax

FLAX IS A BEAUTIFUL cool-weather annual. Preferring temperatures of 50° to 80° Fahrenheit (10° to 26.5° C), it does well in moist, misty locations. If you can grow peas, then you probably can get a flax crop. The traditional European planting date was the Monday after Easter. Harvest would then be in early to mid-July.

What Flax Needs

For flax to thrive, it needs a rich, well-manured, well-tilled soil and full sun. After all danger of frost is past, sow the seeds densely, at a rate of 1 to 1½ grams per square foot. This encourages the growth of a long stem with few branches. The seed germinates within fourteen days.

Flax enjoys a rich soil, but its roots are only 4" to 5" (10 to 12.5 cm) long, so you don't need to till too deeply. You will broadcast the flax seeds and rake them in, so your seed bed should be smooth and the clods well broken. Acccording to your soil type, set up your irrigation system to suit a modest water requirement. Here in California, I have a sandy/clay soil, so I built berms around the level bed and flood-irrigate my flax crop.

Flax matures in 90 to 100 days. If the seed pods mature too fully, you'll harvest plenty of ripe seeds, but the fiber quality will suffer. Pull the crop when the pods are golden about two-thirds of the way up the plant. Bundle the stems in handfuls and bind them. Then, weather permitting, dry them standing in "stooks" in the field. If rain threatens, dry them under cover.

If you ripple the flax (see page 61), it can be stored almost indefinitely and retted (see page 62) at a later date. You'll want to ripple it to make it less attractive to mice. You can also store your flax crop for the long term after it is retted and well dried.

Harvesting Flax

YOU CAN HARVEST BAST FIBERS at least three ways. One approach is to strip the bark and phloem in long ribbons while they're succulent and green. The ribbons are then divided into finer and finer ribbons and used as is.[8] Or you can free the phloem cells from one another by pounding the ribbons, masticating them to remove the thin bark, and rubbing them between your palms. Another process involves scraping the green, coarse fibers off the core. Although it has existed as a hand process for millennia, the method (called "decortication") is now mechanized and used on ramie, hemp, and even some flax. And a third method, most commonly for flax and hemp, involves placing the dried stems in damp conditions for some time until the smaller connective tissues rot away. The stems are then dried again and the fibers are released by a sequence of beating, crushing the pithy core, and "combing" out the remaining bits of core.

Because the phloem runs the entire length of the plant from the roots to the leaves, when it comes time to harvest the crop, the flax is pulled in handfuls from the soil; it's not chopped or cut. These handfuls are bundled, then tied and left to dry in the field. And herein lies a right proper fiber mystery: how do you get the fine spinning fibers from bundles of dry outer skin without breaking them to bits? This requires a closer look.

---

8 This nonspinning method appears globally, being used on a multitude of bast fibers. Truly, spinners and basket makers share a common approach to materials.

Pods containing oil-rich seeds must be removed.

The flax straw with seed pods.

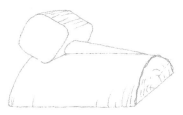

A ripple is a closely set, single row of metal tines.

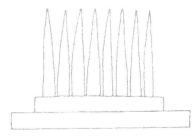

A smooth-faced mallet is used against a curved surface.

Preparing Flax Fiber

ONCE HARVESTED AND DRIED, flax must undergo several processes to separate the spinning fiber from the rest of the stem. It must be rippled, retted, broken, scutched, and hackled.

Rippling or Beating

The first step is to remove the seed pods that grow on the outermost branch tips. These pods contain oil-rich seeds. These seeds are particularly attractive to mice and the oil makes a mess of the retting process, which comes next. Seed removal can be accomplished by one of two methods. The flax straw can be either rippled or beaten. Rippling is a process of drawing the bundled straw through a closely set, single row of tines called a "ripple." The straw passes between the tines and the seed pods don't, so they pop off.

The other method—beating—lightly crushes just the seed pods but not the seeds. The beating can be done with a smooth-faced mallet on a likewise smooth curved surface, such as a log. Place a bundle of straw on the log and lightly pound the tips. Spread a tarp or cloth under the log to catch the seeds.

Continue to treat each bundle of straw in whichever fashion you choose until all the seed heads are broken and removed. At this point, the chaff and seed can be put aside for winnowing. In my experience, it's possible to clean the chaff off the seed with a light puff of breath. After a couple of good puffs, most of the chaff is gone. The rest can be picked out by hand. The seed is used for the next year's crop, oil (known as linseed oil), or animal feed—including human food. It's a delicious inclusion in salads and baking.

After the seed is removed from the flax straw, you have the option of storing the straw as it is (to wait for better conditions) or proceed to the next step: retting. When you consider storage locations and conditions, be aware that flax straw is very flammable.[9]

Flax seeds can be saved for next year's crop, made into linseed oil, or enjoyed right away in a salad.

9 A dear friend attempted to "de-hair" a freshly spun, 900 yd (823 m) skein of linen yarn. She read that industry does this by singeing the fur off dampened yarn with heated rollers. My friend wetted the skein and attempted to pass it through a flame. The fireball was 3 feet tall and only ash remained. This gave her fresh respect for the flammability of flax.

Retting

Retting consists of placing the straw in a damp or wet environment. Bacteria attack the moist material. Some of the softer, thinner plant tissues, such as the cuticle and other connective cells, are consumed first. The goal is to free the phloem from the pithy core before it suffers the same fate as the smaller cells. Managing the retting job takes care and attention—timing is everything.

There are three traditional ways to ret the flax: in a body of still water, such as a pond, tank, or tub; in running water, such as a stream; or with dew or other naturally falling moisture. Naturally-occurring bacterial action begins to work until the smaller connective structures weaken and the gums and glues that hold the phloem in place release their hold: the ultimate goal of retting.

If you have acres of flax to ret and want to do it all at once, you need a large pond deep enough to fully submerge the flax standing upright. This vertical arrangement means temperature and rate of bacterial action is more uniform and better controlled than if the bundles were placed in layers.

If your crop is more the dooryard size, your tank can be a child's plastic pool, a 55-gallon (207 l) barrel, or a 32-gallon (121 l) trashcan. The point is, you need some container that will take the length of straw you have and keep all of it wet. And the process goes more smoothly if you can keep the water temperature pretty constant.

Stream retting takes place in running water. The bundled, tied flax is set in flowing water where bacterial action is slower. The water may be colder than a nearby pond or tank, and some of the bacteria are carried away. Retting in a living stream environment is challenging; it may even be illegal. Check with your local authorities. The effluent from flax retting is not toxic on its own, but the bacteria involved in the process remove oxygen from the water. In a pond, they may remove all the oxygen. In running water, the bacteria can't use up all the oxygen, but they do have an impact on stream dwellers—fish, amphibians, and water plants. A process with results similar to stream retting can be managed by letting a low volume of water enter the retting pool or tank and, likewise, the same volume permitted to run off onto the ground. So why would you want to do stream retting? The process takes longer, but the resulting fiber is lighter in color and silkier.

Whether in stream or pond, flax straw has a tendency to float, so it must be weighted down. Refrigerator racks and bricks, or wooden pallets and well-placed rocks, will work to keep the bundles well below the surface and thoroughly wet. Large-scale flax operations put the flax straw in crates, which make handling efficient and also keeps the bundles submerged.

Retting occurs faster with warmer water temperatures. At 85° Fahrenheit (29.5° Celsius), the flax may be fully retted in three days. In just three and a half days at the same temperature, the flax may be seriously over-retted and the staple length compromised. Drop the temperature to 40° Fahrenheit (4.5° Celsius), and retting might take weeks. Stream retting may require even longer, perhaps months.

A word about another aspect of retting: pond or tank retting can have a "nose," a piquancy that is difficult to tolerate in tight quarters. Your apartment housemates or suburban neighbors may be glad if the retting is quick.

Slower retting can result in greater control over the process and better-quality fiber. Dew retting takes place over a long period of time, often during the winter season.

The flax straw bundles are left in an open area, such as a field or meadow, to be rained and snowed upon. The bundles must be kept moist and turned from time to time. This gradual and labor-intensive process works best in damp climates. Even with the best attention, the color of flax processed by dew retting is uneven.

Retting skirts the possibility of complete decomposition. If taken too far, the gum that holds the ultimates in place is consumed. When this happens, the fiber is reduced to the length of the ultimate cell: maybe 1" (2.5 cm) long. During retting, you must check the fiber frequently to see how far the process has progressed. You do so by breaking a piece of straw and seeing if the fibers make a brushy fringe around the pith core. If they can be pulled back in long strips, then it's time to stop the retting, pull the flax from the water, and rinse and dry it. You'll see that "just right" point when you bend the straw to breaking. The pith should break and you should be able to peel the long fibers back off the pith. If the pith and the phloem both break, that means that retting has gone either not enough or too much. Too early and the break will be a sharp cut edge; phloem and pith will both break. Too late and the break will be furry; the pith will break and the phloem will be too degraded to hold the full staple length.

Stop the retting process when the fibers can be pulled back in long strips.

Breaking and Scutching

After the bundles of flax are dried, the next step in separating and removing the pith from the fiber is to crush the core. A flax break is a tool used to crush and reduce the core to shorter lengths. The break looks like a heavy pair of scissors on legs. The "cutting edge" is made up of rounded wooden slats offset from one another so that the upper slats slide between and next to the lower slats. The flax straw bundle is placed between the "jaws" of the break, then the jaws are brought together. The bundle is worked from end to end, breaking and crushing the core. When all goes well, the core begins to part from the long fibers as it is chopped into short lengths.

The core is further removed from the bundle in a process known as "scutching," using a scutching stake and sword. The boardlike stake is notched at the top. The wooden scutching sword is flat on one side and beveled on the other. It isn't particularly sharp. The tip of the flax bundle rests in the notch while the wooden sword is brought down against the straw and scutching stake to scrape away the pith and remaining bits of cuticle trash. The bundle is worked from the tip to beyond the middle and then turned to work from the other end to the middle.

| BREAKING | SCUTCHING |

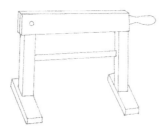

A flax break works like a heavy pair of scissors on legs.

A scrutching stake and sword are used to further remove the core.

The "jaws" are brought together to break and crush the core within a straw bundle.

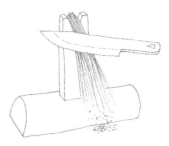

The sword is brought down against the straw to scrape away pith and cuticle trash.

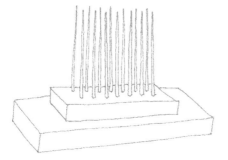

A hackle is used to separate the fiber from the "skin."

Cross-section of wool combs and hackle pins.

Hackling

After scutching, a good deal of the pith should be on the ground and "ribbons" and flax fibers should remain in your hand. The ribbons are fibers that are still attached to the cuticle. You need a tool to separate the fiber from the "skin." That tool is called a hackle (or heckle or hatchel), and it's basically a large comb.

Hackles are similar to wool combs with one important difference. Wool combs are used to remove shorter fibers from the staple and open up lightly felted fibers. Their pins are smooth, round in cross section, and sharp only on the pointed tip. Flax hackles, on the other hand, are used to pierce and separate the flax fibers and ribbons, and the dregs of the woody core. Hackle pins are square in cross-section and made sharp on their four corners. They are drawn to a needle point, clustered into a round or square pattern, and mounted in a sturdy block. Hackles can come in sets: fine, medium, and coarse pins. Their density of set and pin height are designed to work the bundles of flax through to finer and finer fibers without sacrificing fiber length.

Two sizes of hackles.

Hackles are a necessary tool for the flax spinner, especially for one who spins line flax, and here's why. Purchased flax is available in three forms: strick, sliver, and tow. Strick is a long ponytail that has been processed as above: rippled, broken, scutched, and hackled. It is also known as "line" flax and it makes a smooth, sleek yarn. The stuff that is hackled out of long line fiber is called tow. Tow is the short, irregular leftovers and yields a coarser, more textured yarn. Longer fibers can be rehackled and spun like line with good result.

Let's take a closer look at the steps involved in hackling to get some sense of how it works.

To begin, clamp the hackle to a sturdy table, with good ventilation. This process should preferably take place outside because of the extensive dust and debris. The hackle should be just at your waist height or a bit lower.

Stand so that when your arms are fully extended you can't touch the hackle pins. This keeps you from needing that tetanus booster.

Determine which is the leaf end and which is the root. Both ends are tapered, but the leaf end has a long taper, the root much shorter. The fibers on the leaf end are finer than the root fibers too.

With the leaf end of the strick pointing at the hackle, hold it in your dominant hand about a third of the way down from the leaf end.

Flip the very tip, 1" to 2" (2.5 to 5 cm), of the strick onto the points of the hackles and pull the fiber straight downward towards the base of the hackles.

Pull the strick toward you until the fibers clear the hackle.

Strick (top), also known as "line" flax, makes a smooth yarn; *tow* (bottom) yields a coarser, more textured yarn.

Clamp the hackle at waist height and stand far enough away that you can't touch the hackle pins.

ROOT   LEAF

*The **root end** (left) has a shorter taper than the **leaf end** (right).*

64

HOW TO HACKLE FLAX

Hold the strick about a third of the way down from the leaf end.

Flip the tip of the strick onto the hackle.

Pull straight down toward the base of the hackle.

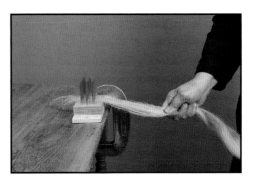

Pull the strick toward you until the fibers clear the hackle.

Flip the ends of the strick onto the hackle points again, this time just a bit closer to your hand. Pull the fiber straight downward to the base of the hackles, then pull toward you, clearing the hackle.

Continue to ease your way into the body of the strick in small increments, making sure that you keep your hands away from the hackle pins and that you pull down to the base of the hackle and then pull towards yourself.

When you get halfway down the strick, turn it and begin to work the root end in the same way you worked the leaf end, in small increments.

HACKLE BASICS

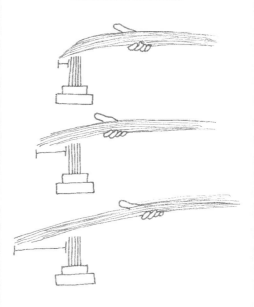

Ease your way to the midpoint of the strick, flipping more of the fiber on the hackle with each pass.

When you get to the middle, turn the strick around and repeat for the other end.

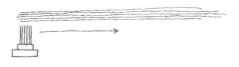

Work until the strick is uniformly open, limp, and soft.

Tow will be left in the hackle with each pass.

Rehackling will produce shorter and shorter staple lengths.

Work until you get to the "waist," or center, of the strick. The strick will feel more open, limp, and soft.[10] You're now ready to dress a distaff and spin.

If at any time you can't pull the fiber through the hackles, stop. Lift the fiber straight up to remove it from the hackles, then begin again. It could be that your strick is too large to be handled well. Separate it in half and try again. This time, don't move so rapidly down the strick. Relax and encourage a rhythm as you flick, pull down, pull through, and move down the strick. It probably got difficult to pull because you got too much of the dense part of the strick on the hackle—you took "too big a bite."

Hackling opens the strick and makes it less dense; the fibers flow freely. It also removes the short fibers. As you change hackles, you can improve the fineness of your fiber. But you don't need a set of hackles to vastly improve the quality of your yarn. If you have only one hackle, you will still make your spinning chore much easier by hackling the fiber before spinning it.

And this is why: the strick flax contains pectin, which becomes sticky in damp conditions, such as those common to warehouses, foggy mornings, or Midwestern summers. As the humidity drops, the sticky pectin acts like a glue; the flax fibers adhere to one other. This means that when you first purchase your strick, it has most likely seen some wet/dry cycles since it was last hackled.

10 As you reach the middle of the strick, you'll find longer and longer fibers left on the hackle. It's a heartache to see good fiber pulled out, but it comes with the territory. You can re-hackle the longer stuff, remove the shorter tow, and spin nice yarn from both.

It may see more at your studio before you're able to spin it.[11] The hard truth is that if you're bitten by the line flax bug and fall in love, you'll need at least one hackle.

Another truth is that you shouldn't hackle more than you can comfortably spin in a given time frame. Huge, be-ribboned, bouffant distaves full of flax are magnificent. But seriously, can you spin it all before the next wet/dry cycle? Do you really want to rehackle the fiber on the distaff before you can get back to spinning? Unless you are working for a period piece, hackle only what you are going to use in the immediate future. In the end, this will save you time.

The tow fiber from hackling can be rehackled and sorted to staple lengths.

The stuff longer than 6" or 7" (15 or 18 cm) can be spun in a similar manner to line flax and, in some situations, can be ultrafine and high quality. Tow fibers shorter than 6" (15 cm) can be carded on handcards, rolled into flax rolags, and spun into coarser useful yarns. Specific carders for tow have what looks like short stocky nails in the place of bent wire. But you can also card tow on standard wool handcarders, especially if you haven't used them to card grease fleece. If you plan to do a lot of tow carding, you may want to delegate a particular pair of handcards for this purpose. Because your rolags will contain a variety of staple lengths, your yarn won't be absolutely consistent or slub-free.

Tow yarns were used traditionally for the myriad bags and canvas items needed to sustain

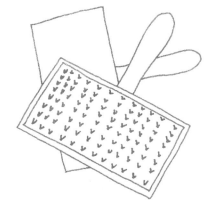

Rehackled tow laid in staple bundles.

Use tow carders for tow fibers that are shorter than 6" (15 cm) long.

farm and household, thus the term "tow sack" for bags made from tow flax yarn. They also serve well as table mats, dish and face cloths, market bags, mug rugs, and bathmats—but not hot pads, please, as flax is quite flammable.

---

11 During a fine flax spinning competition, I got the bright idea to spritz my distaff thinking that would make the yarn finer and stronger. For a few moments the line drafted very well. Then breezes blew, the sun shone, and the fiber on my distaff petrified—it completely glued together. *Lesson: When competing, don't venture into untried technology.*

The Lesser Flax of Life

Not all flax is rippled, broken, scutched, and hackled. Only line flax gets that special attention.

Some flax is scraped from the green stem in a process known as decortication. The broken fiber is treated, rinsed, and dried. The staple length for decorticated bast fibers ranges from 3" (7.5 cm) to 5" or 6" (12.5 or 15 cm). This decorticated fiber is sometimes available in carded sliver form. As with all machine-prepared materials, there is a "nap" or a better end and a not-so-good end from which to spin. Try one end, and then turn it around to try the other end. You'll soon know which end is the easiest to work.

Because this preparation contains a variety of staple lengths and perhaps some remains of the pithy core as well, the yarn spun from it will be neither consistent nor even. It will be a "character" yarn. Very fine yarns may prove difficult to produce.

If the material has been dyed, you'll need to be alert to gumminess. Dyeing is a wet process and flax contains pectin, as I've noted before, which becomes sticky with moisture. Some decorticated flax is degummed, which can remove most if not all the pectin, but some is not degummed. Check the sliver before you purchase it and if it's dense and doesn't draft freely, you'll know why. You always have the option to re-card the material into rolags, which should make your yarn more consistent and spinning this preparation much faster.

Another form of flax is said to have been "cottonized." This fiber has a staple length of about 1" (2.5 cm), which is similar to cotton. It is industrially carded and spun following the same systems used for cotton. It is available in carded sliver blends as well as carded yarns. Its great advantage is that the label says "linen" or "flax" and thus a premium price can be applied.

Because of its short staple length, cottonized flax has a short drafting zone. Depending on the condition of the flax fiber and the size of the yarn spun, the sliver can draft freely or produce a yarn something more akin to random potatoes in pantyhose (but on a small scale).

Carded decorticated flax ranges from 3" (7.5 cm) to 5" or 6" (12.5 to 15 cm) long.

"Cottonized" flax has a staple length of about 1" (25 cm), which is similar to cotton.

Spinning Flax

A LOT OF EFFORT GOES INTO FIBER preparation for flax, but that's all behind us now. We're close to working this lovely fiber. I'll first cover spinning with premium, long, line fiber, then move to spinning rehackled line fiber. Spinning carded tow is next, followed by spinning commercial sliver. As for tools, we'll begin with the treadled wheel and conclude with the spindle.

When spinning flax, the first goal is to manage long-line fiber without disarranging it. Remember, the fiber is some 30" (76 cm) long and crushable. And if there's any moisture in your hands, you can make a glued-up mess of it. Clearly, you'll need help to support the fiber and keep it orderly. This is what distaves are for.

The Distaff

The distaff can be as simple as a peg or nail in the wall or overhead beam, or as complex as a fully articulated and adjustable freestanding device that can be raised and lowered to fit any length of flax. In the European tradition, there are beautiful and varied forms of distaves—truncheon, comb, basket, cage, paddle, and staff. Often, the distaff was a courting gift, something to show the prospective bride how skilled, dedicated, and resourceful her beau could be.

The **freestanding distaff** is typically a single upright pole with a substantial base and perhaps short legs. It can have adjustable elements to permit the staff head to start at the full height for the longest fibers and gradually lower as the longest fibers are removed.[12]

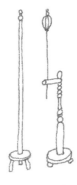

Distaves have many forms, such as tuncheon, basket, comb, cage and paddle distaff.

With the distaff tied to a chair, you have both hands free to draft.

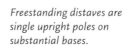

Freestanding distaves are single upright poles on substantial bases.

---

12 You really don't want to spin with your hands and arms above your shoulders. It will be tough on you.

The top of this style of distaff has a knob or finial to which you tie your flax. There may be a lantern or cage shape below the knob, or the upright may be topped with a comb or basket. Of note is that it can be moved away from the wheel's orifice at least the staple length while you sit back in your chair and adjust the work for comfort and good light. It also permits you to use both hands to draft the fiber.

Many wheels are made with distaff attached to the wheel frame.[13] The chief advantage to a **wheel-mounted distaff** is that it limits the spinner's "footprint": the spinning wheel is the only item, besides the spinner and chair, that takes any floor space. In tight working areas, space can be an issue. However, consider that this distaff doesn't hold the fiber high enough or sufficiently far away from the wheel's orifice. The elements of this setup are just too closely coupled. This type of distaff is seen in many paintings. However, personal experience proves that this isn't an efficient or effective setup for spinning prime flax. Shorter fibers, tow, or rehackled line can, however, be managed on a wheel-set distaff.

Spindle-spinning line flax calls for a **belt distaff**—a stick that slips into a belt around your waist. Like its longer cousin, this distaff features a simple knob or structure on top of a straight staff. The staff is stuck in your belt so that it's cradled by your nondominant-hand shoulder. The staff should be firmly cinched so that the lower 5" to 7" (12.5 to 18 cm) fall inside the hollow of your hipbone. The top of the staff should rest in the "valley" between your shoulder muscle and your collarbone. This setup puts the bulk of the fiber over your head.

A wheel-mounted distaff requires less floor space.

A belt distaff is used with a spindle.

When the belt distaff is properly worn, you have two hands free to manage the spindle and the drafting zone, and still be able to walk about, bend over, and chase kids.

---

13 This setup may be a remnant of the "put out" factory system when hand spinners spun their yarn at home and sold it to textile manufacturers.

Handheld distaves are useful on line flax that is considerably less than 36" (91.5 cm) long.[14] The handheld distaff is a straight, shorter pole that's about 18" to 22" (45.5 to 56 cm) long and has a nob on one end and a handle on the other. The hand holding the distaff helps to manage the drafting zone from time to time.

There are a number of ways to make an even simpler distaff. For a towel distaff, just lay the hackled flax on one long edge of the towel and roll the line up in the towel, leaving a couple of inches of flax exposed on one end of the towel "burrito." The towel can be placed in your lap, over your shoulder, or on a table beside you.

You can mount a hook in the ceiling or a peg in a beam or post, and spin line flax tied to that peg. The fiber bundle can be lowered if you have allowed a couple of yards of ribbon to tie it to the peg.

You can also tie a freshly hackled strick to your belt at your back waist. Bring the fiber up over one shoulder and, presto, *you* are the distaff. This method works best with small bundles of fibers that are quickly spun.

14 The "Statue of Liberty" pose for line spinning is not recommended.

WAYS TO USE DISTAVES

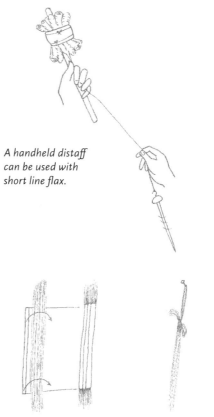

A handheld distaff can be used with short line flax.

Roll hackled flax in a towel for a simple distaff.

Tie the strick to a peg in a beam or post.

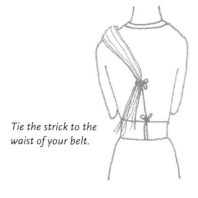

Tie the strick to the waist of your belt.

Dressing the Distaff

There are many ways to dress a distaff, depending on its style and the length and quality of the fiber.

Simple Straight Distaff

The straight distaff is basically a pole that rests in a base, is held in your hand, or slips into your belt. To dress the straight distaff, lay your freshly hackled flax on a flat surface. Determine which end is the root and which is the flower/leaf end. Both ends of the fiber bundle are tapered. The root end has thicker fibers and is more abruptly tapered. You'll need about 2½ to 3 yards (2.3 to 2.7 m) of smooth satin ribbon—about ⅛" to ½" (3 mm to 1.3 cm) wide—for long line and about 2 yards (1.8 m) for shorter, perhaps rehackled, line on a hand-held staff. This is the most practical and easily rehackled way to dress a distaff.

To begin, tie the flax about a third of the way down from the flower end, making the tie in the middle of the length of ribbon. Make the tie snug—just how tight is a judgment call. If the tie is too firm, the fiber will be snagged by the ribbon and cease flowing; too loose, and it all comes down at once. Be prepared to retie your flax as you spin.

Use the ribbon to tie the bundle to the nob at the top of the distaff.

Crisscross the two ends of the ribbon around both the staff and the fiber to secure them.

Leave the last 4" to 6" (10 to 15 cm) of the root end unbound.—If you have extra ribbon, use it up by tying it into a big bow. Your lovely line flax is now ready to be spun.

DRESSING A SIMPLE STRAIGHT DISTAFF

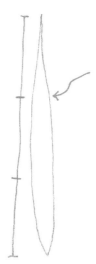  

Tie the strick one-third of the way down from the flower end.

Use ribbon to tie the strick to the top of the distaff.

Crisscross the two ends of the ribbon around the fiber and staff.

Simple Comb Distaff

A new straw broom set into a Christmas tree stand makes a dandy economical comb-style distaff.

Set the broom into the stand with the handle down, straw head pointing up.

Use a couple of yards (1.8 m) of satin ribbon to tie your flax a third of the way down the fiber, near the flower end, to the neck of the broom. Don't tie the fiber bundle close and snug to the neck; instead, give it a couple of extra inches (5 cm) of ribbon, and then tie to the broom.

Flip the end of flax "tail" over the bottom cut edge of the bristles and use the ends of the ribbon tied to gently secure the end of the flaxen tail to that face of the broom. Finish with a bow to keep the ends of the ribbon out of the drafting area.

As the longer fibers are consumed in yarn, untie the bundle to allow more length between the tied bundle of fibers and the broom neck, effectively lowering the end of the "ponytail," then retie to the broom neck.

Secure the broom handle into the stand so the straw head points up.

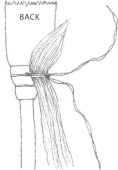

BACK

Use satin ribbon to tie the strick about one-third of the way down from the flower end.

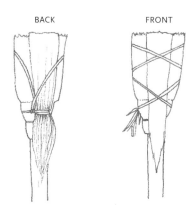

BACK   FRONT

Flip the end of the flax over the bristles and secure with ribbon.

MANAGING SHORT FIBERS

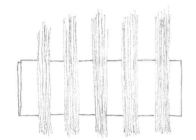

Lay short fibers on a smooth linen towel.

Roll the towel and tie it onto a handheld distaff.

Using Odds and Ends

Rehackled fiber and fiber that has been pulled from the first hackling can be high-quality stuff, just shorter. It should be set aside and graded into staple lengths. The longer fiber can be dressed simply as previously described. But you'll want to use a different technique for the shorter fiber.

To begin, lay short fibers crosswise on a smooth, folded linen guest towel, placing rehackled tufts side by side until the towel is full or until you run out of tufts.

Roll the towel onto a handheld straight distaff and tie it in place at the top and bottom, making sure that a good length of tuft sticks from out the bottom of the roll.

Carded rolags can replace the tufts, which is a handy stunt for rolags of any fiber—no need to make joins!

With your distaff dressed, you're ready to adjust your wheel and begin spinning. (Cheering from the peanut gallery!)

Spinning Line
Flax on a Wheel

The wheel adjustments for spinning flax are opposite those for cotton. For cotton, we need high twist and little take-up; for flax, we need less twist and strong take-up.

Flax yarn is like wire. Relax the yarn, and it hops off the hooks looking for something to grab. Remember that flax is strong. Most likely, the yarn will be the last thing to break, after snagging a nearby knob or protuberance. You want to wind this stuff into a firm package on the bobbin—otherwise the yarn slides all over the place and lost ends are impossible to find. And a firm package is easier to wind off. Therefore, you want to adjust your wheel for positive take-up.

The way to increase take-up on a double-drive wheel is to put the drive cord around the flyer and bobbin whorls of the greatest difference in size; in other words, big flyer whorl, small bobbin whorl.

The way to increase take-up on a flyer lead single-drive, or scotch tension, wheel is to increase the tension on the bobbin brake. You may need to increase drive cord tension just a bit, too. But go too far, and your treadling effort will likewise increase.

The single-drive bobbin lead wheel already has plenty of take-up but, if you need more, you can increase tension on the flyer brake strap or cord. This adjustment achieves large effect for small changes.

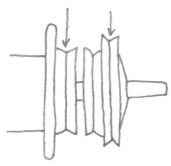

For double-drive wheels, put the drive cord around the bobbin and flyer whorls of the greatest difference in size.

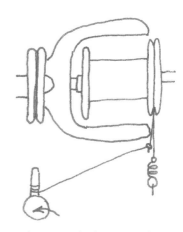

For scotch-tension wheels, increase the tension on the bobbin brake.

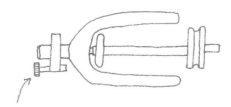

For single-drive bobbin-lead wheels, increase the tension on the flyer brake strap or cord.

Remember to oil your wheel!

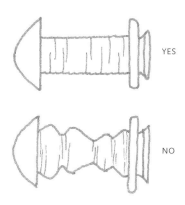

YES

NO

For best results, build a smooth cylinder of yarn on the bobbin.

1-2"

Place the distaff a staple length away from the orifice.

Do remember to oil your wheel.

Because line flax has such a generous staple length, the yarn won't need as much twist as a cotton or wool yarn of the same grist would need to hold the yarn together. So, you can either treadle slower or use the mechanical advantage of the larger drive whorl on the flyer. You may be spinning a gossamer yarn, but it won't take a lot of twist to make it.

And finally, as a general rule of thumb, be scrupulous about changing the yarn onto different hooks frequently and regularly. Build a solid cylinder on your bobbin made up of many thin layers of yarn so your bobbin will unwind with grace.

You now have two hands to draft your fiber because your fiber hand has been replaced by a distaff.

Place the distaff in a comfortable position. The tip of the "ponytail" needs to be a staple length away from the orifice—somewhere between 20" to 40" (51 to 101.5 cm). It also needs to be a couple of inches (a few centimeters) higher than the wheel orifice. If you can, set the distaff to one side of you so that you can draft across your body.

You can either make a leader (see page 80) or tie an already-spun leader onto the bobbin.

If you're going to tie a leader onto the bobbin, make it a yard or two (.9 to 1.8 m) long and make it a fine two-ply cellulose yarn.[15] Tie the leader to the bobbin and thread it over the hooks and out the orifice, then lay 18" to 20" (45.5 to 51 cm) of leader against the fiber.

To begin, pinch off the twist at some place just south of the beard, and treadle a couple of times to ensure that you have plenty of twist available to join the leader to the fiber on the distaff. Stop treadling. Open your pinched fingers, permitting the twist to run up the yarn and into the distaff fiber. It should entangle some fibers and permit you to pull more fibers straight down.

Begin to slowly treadle. Moisten the fingers of your wheel-side hand and pinch the contact point between the fibers and the leader.

Use your fiber hand to reach up to where the fibers are coming out of the tip of the "beard" and pull straight down.

Without opening the fingers of either hand, slide your wheel-side hand towards your fiber hand, moistening and smoothing the yarn as the twist runs into it.

When your hands nearly touch, reach up with your fiber hand and pull down another length of unspun, sheer fiber.

Continue to use your wheel hand to feed the spun yarn onto the flyer and bobbin without opening or letting twist between your hands, while moving your fiber-side hand in tandem with the wheel hand when winding on.

What you're doing is a full-worsted draft.[16] There should be twist ahead, or to the wheel side, of the hand closest to the spinning wheel. There should be no twist between your hands. The hand closest to the wheel is the "contact" point where twist meets the drafted fiber; your other hand manages the drafting zone between your two hands and into the distaff fiber.

Remember that the drafting zone is as long as the staple length. If you let any twist escape behind your fiber-side hand, the size of your yarn will increase rapidly.

This type of spinning progresses as you pull down on the tip of the distaff "beard" with your fiber hand, slide your wheel hand toward the fiber hand, wind on with both hands, then pull down again with your fiber hand. In time, this will assume a gentle rhythm, but I can't tell you just how much to pull down and just how much to wind on. With experience, you'll learn how far you need to draft for the yarn you want to make, based on the condition of the fiber and how it was prepared.

If your yarn is too thin, you'll need to grab more fibers with each draft; if your yarn is too thick, you'll want to grab fewer fibers and pull them down a greater distance. It may take a few drafts to change (up or down) the size of the yarn.

Go slowly at first until you get a feel for it. Later, you can speed up.

---

15 I've found that cellulose fiber joins to cellulose yarn easier than protein to cellulose. See if it works for you.

16 You are working from a worsted preparation, all the short stuff is removed and the fibers are parallel. You are drafting without any twist. The twist always is ahead of your lead, or wheel-side, hand.

SPINNING FROM A DISTAFF

Lay 18" to 20" (45.5 to 51 cm) of yarn against the distaff.

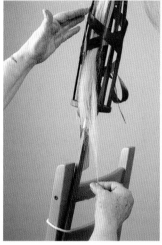

Permit the twist to run up the yarn and into the distaff fiber.

Pinch the contact point between the fibers and leader.

Use your fiber hand to pull straight down on the fiber.

Slide your wheel-side hand toward your fiber hand, moistening and smoothing the yarn as the twist runs into it.

Reach up with your fiber hand and pull down another length of fiber.

How to Make a Leader

Pull down 18" to 20" (45.5 to 51 cm) of fiber from the bottom of the fiber on the distaff.

Roll the fiber down your leg, using the palm of your hand placed on that tip of fiber.

Pull down more fiber and roll more twist into the forming yarn. Remember to roll only down your leg, not up and down. Try to make a fairly fine smooth yarn. It's more important that the yarn be fine than particularly consistent or smooth.

When you have 24" to 28" (61 to 71 cm) of yarn, thread the orifice from the flyer arm side and pull the tip of the yarn through.

Tie or wrap the yarn onto the first hook of the flyer. You can now treadle the wheel and get more twist to make longer yarn. Just don't pull on the yarn—it will slip off the hook and out the orifice and you'll need to rethread it through the orifice.

Once you have a generous amount of yarn between you and the wheel, untie or unwrap the yarn from the first hook, pass it over the first few hooks, then tie or overlap it onto the bobbin. Once there are a couple of layers of yarn, it will hold.

Pull 18" to 20" (45.5 to 51 cm) of fiber down from the distaff.

Use the palm of your hand to roll the fiber along your leg.

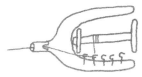

When you have 24" to 28" (61 to 71 cm) of yarn, thread it through the orifice and tie it to a hook, then treadle.

Untie the yarn from the hook and wrap it onto the bobbin.

MAKING JOINS

Lay the broken end against the distaff.

Moisten the contact point.

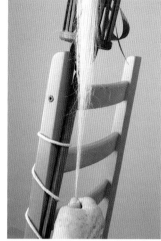

Pull down the new fiber, smoothing and joining the old yarn to the new.

Making Joins

To rejoin a broken yarn to the fiber, lay the broken end of the yarn against the distaff, allowing about 10" to 18" (25.5 to 45.5 cm) of overlap.

Moisten the bottom edge of the fiber that contacts the yarn.

Pull down new fiber, smoothing and joining the old yarn to the new.

Spin the fiber wet. Keep in mind that pectin activated by moisture helps to smooth the surface of the yarn. Traditionally, spinners would moisten their fingers with spit or dip them in a bowl of water placed within easy reach. Many opinionated spinners feel that beer not only wets your whistle, but adds enzymatic action to your saliva. It certainly reduces stress.

Spinning Line Flax
on a Handspindle

You'll find many advantages to spinning flax on a spindle: you're free to stand, sit, or move about, and the spindle is much lighter to carry and store. The freedom of movement is unequalled.

Before you begin, a few words about spindle design and flax spinning are appropriate. Flax is a stiff fiber and even fine flax yarns resist twist. This affects the way your spindles behave. Flax spindles need more "cast," or momentum, to overcome the stiffness of the fiber. This means that they typically weigh more than you would expect for the given size of yarn.

You could spin a fine line flax yarn on a tahkli, but it wouldn't be efficient. First of all, flax doesn't need the high twist that tahklis can deliver. Second, most tahklis don't weigh much, and would therefore require significantly more twiddling than if you were spinning a cotton yarn of the same size.

Flax spindles don't need to put in twist rapidly. Therefore, their shafts can be thicker at the tip and less vulnerable to breakage—the spindles are more robust than those used for cotton.

However, the spindle must manage the wiry quality of freshly spun flax yarn, which can be controlled by the method used to wind the yarn onto your spindle. Wiry yarn is best wound on with a rapid traverse. In other words, the yarn is laid on the spindle shaft at a low angle. As you wind on, move the yarn rapidly from side to side while turning the spindle. The yarn package on the spindle ends up pointed on both ends with a rounded belly.

The tip of a flax spindle is thicker and less apt to break.

Wind the yarn on the spindle at a low angle.

TRADITIONAL FLAX SPINDLES

Two whorls help support the lively yarn and allow for a longer cast.

The Egyptian spindle has an extra-long shaft and a small-diameter whorl for better stability at high speeds.

This forms a side-delivery package.[17] Unwind it from the side, not over the spindle tip.

Another way to deal with the wiry flax yarn is evidenced by two traditional flax spindles: the double whorl and the Egyptian high-whorl hook top. Two whorls help support lively yarn

---

17 End-feed delivery packages, such as cone-shaped spindle cops and weaving shuttle pirns, are extremely challenging with flax yarns.

and keep it orderly. The extra whorl also adds mass to the spindle, giving it a longer cast.

The Egyptian high whorl, hook-top spindle is seen in hieroglyphs and ancient murals. It has an extra-long shaft for its small diameter whorl. This combination gives it better stability at high speeds as well as generous storage area for wiry flax yarns.

Both spindles share a hooked top, which lets you run the spindle either down or up your thigh to initiate twist. This process is vastly more effective than "twiddling" the spindle with your thumb and index finger!

What's best for you is the spindle with which you are currently comfortable, one that has a reasonably long shaft so you can wind on at a long angle, and one with some weight to it.

Tip: *You'll want to spin a fine flax yarn. The easiest to spin is a yarn the size of carpet* thread. *Fine yarns give you time to draft them and time to learn to manage the spindle. Remember that flax is very strong—you'll have a difficult time breaking it between your hands—and it doesn't need a lot of twist.*

Spindle Spinning with a Distaff

The considerable staple length of flax means that you'll need some sort of distaff, just as for spinning flax on a wheel. To spin the longest line flax, you'll want to use a belt distaff that lets you use both hands to draft (similar to spinning on a wheel). Put the distaff on your left hip and shoulder if you're right-handed; put it on your right hip and shoulder if you're left-handed.

Join up with either a leader or directly as explained for wheel spinning (see pages 80–81). Remember that you're spinning a worsted draft with no twist between your nondominant hand

---

USING A BELT DISTAFF

Pull some fiber down with your nondominant hand.

Precede the twist up the fiber with your dominant hand.

Draw down another length of fiber.

and the fiber, and no twist between your non-dominant and dominant hand. The twist occurs between your dominant hand and the spindle.

Pull some fiber down from the distaff with your nondominant hand.

Start the spindle rotating, slowly at first. Wet your master-hand fingers. Precede the twist up the fiber with your master hand, moistening and smoothing the yarn as it forms.

When your master hand and non-master hand meet, draw down another length of fiber from the distaff. Check your spindle to see that it is still rotating in the right direction and wet your master hand fingers and precede the twist up the fiber.

Wind on using a rapid and long traverse.

There are a lot of details to manage when spinning line flax on a belt distaff. Soon all the essential parts—keeping the spindle turning, smoothing the twist with your master hand, and pulling straight down with your non-master hand—become second nature and is grand fun. It also draws a crowd.

Using a Handheld Distaff

Truncheon or "stick" distaves work well with shorter and rehackled line flax. The distaff needs to be about 5" (12.5 cm) longer than the flax staple length to give you plenty of room to hold it. It also should feel comfortable in your hand, be lightweight, and permit you to hold it with your ring and pinky fingers only. Your thumb and index fingers will be pinching off the twist to keep it from entering the fiber on the distaff.

Join up your spindle to the distaff using a 2-ply cotton or linen leader tied to your spindle. Place the 12" (30.5 cm) leader against the distaff. Hold the distaff in your non-master hand (i.e., your fiber hand), and pinch off the twist

coming from the spindle with your non-master hand index finger and thumb.

Start the spindle rotating slowly at first. Moisten your dominant-hand (i.e., spindle-hand) fingers, then use your spindlehand thumb and index finger to pinch off the twist right next to your fiber-hand thumb and index finger.

Open your fiber-hand fingers and pull down some fiber with your spindle hand.

Close your fiber-hand fingers and slide your spindle-hand fingers along the fibers, smoothing and moistening the yarn as it forms under them.

When your spindle-hand fingers reach the fiber-hand fingers, moisten them again, then pinch the twist off at the fiber-hand point, open the fiber-hand fingers, pull down more fiber with the spindle hand, and close the spindle-hand fingers to prevent the twist from climbing into the fiber on the distaff.

With the truncheon handheld distaff, the pull-down is managed with the spindle hand; otherwise the spinning essentials are the same.

If you're spinning rehackled flax that's less than 12" (30.5 cm) long, you can place it crosswise on a wide ribbon, woven inkle band, or folded towel, then roll the towel onto the stick distaff (see page 77). Snug the rolled towel against the distaff with ties or ribbons. Doing so lets you spin shorter, but otherwise nice, fibers into a smooth worsted yarn following the same steps.

Spindle Spinning with No Distaff

A rough and ever-ready distaff is your own svelte form. You can hackle a length of line flax and tie it about a third of the way from the flower end with 1 to 1½ yards (.9 to 1.4 m) of satin ribbon.

USING A HANDHELD DISTAFF

Hold the distaff in your fiber hand, and use your nondominant hand to pinch off the twist coming from the spindle.

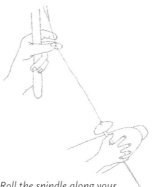

Roll the spindle along your leg to start it spinning.

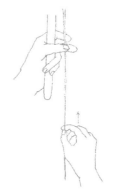

Slide your spindle hand along the fibers to your fiber hand.

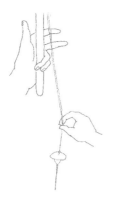

Pull down some fiber with your spindle hand.

Slide your spindle hand up the forming yarn until you reach your fiber hand.

BODY DISTAFF

Tie the ribbon to the center back of a belt around your waist.

Use both hands to draft with a belt or free-standing distaff.

Tie the ribbon to your belt at your center back. Bring the fiber up over your nondominant-hand shoulder and adjust the ribbon length to put the ends of the flax at a comfortable working spot.

Use both hands to draft as if you had a belt distaff or were sitting at the wheel with a free-standing distaff.

Spinning Flax Tow

Tow is the dregs or noil left in the hackles after processing line, and there tends to be plenty of it. In the first century AD, Pliny the Elder observed that the ratio of dry flax straw to finished spinning fiber is 50 to 15. Traditional use for this plentiful material was for bagging and canvas because there was always need for sturdy fabrics. Tow, by nature, is of irregular staple length and quality; it's coarse and stiff, with little elasticity. If you take care to sort it by staple length and remove the tangles or neps, tow can produce attractive and functional yarns.

Spinning tow from carded rolags may remind you of spinning carded adult mohair or the long wools. Be careful to handle the rolags as lightly as you can. They crush easily and if your hands are damp, they'll become compressed and no longer draft freely.

Despite the fact that tow is spun from a carded form, it's a good idea to spin with a worsted draw. The loops and bouclé effects that result from a woolen or semi-woolen draft make snagging a significant problem for linen yarns. The individual fibers are strong and, if snagged, may not break, but instead pull the yarn out of the structure. Smooth flax yarns are the goal.

To begin, hold the rolag lightly with your non-dominant hand and overlap it with the leader.

Let a bit of twist contact the end of the rolag, moisten the contact point, and pull a length of unspun fiber from the tip of the rolag.

With your moistened dominant hand, slide your thumb and forefinger up the drafted fiber just ahead of the twist.

Treadle or turn the spindle slowly at first as you pull out more unspun fiber and precede the twist up the fiber. Let some yarn wind onto your wheel or wind onto the spindle as needed.

The key to spinning tow fiber is to spin it damp, like line flax. But take care not to get the rolags wet, just moisten the the yarn ahead of the drafting zone.

Also, you want to spin a fine yarn. Thick flax yarns are tricky to make consistent. They tend to contain large slubs and thin spots.

Spinning Flax Tow with a Distaff

Spinning tow from rolags mounted on a distaff is a quick and easy way to build confidence to spin other, perhaps less familiar, forms of flax.

To begin, lay the rolags crosswise on a smooth towel or wide ribbon.

Roll the towel or ribbon into a bundle, then tie it onto a straight shaft distaff. Use extra ties to hold it to the staff.

This careful handling prevents you from crushing, disarranging, or dampening the rolags before you get the opportunity to spin them. There are two additional advantages: spinning rolags from a distaff means you don't have to make many joins—and you have two hands free to draft and smooth the yarn.

Joins are usually not a serious problem with this method, but if you do need to make one, treat it similarly to the joins for line flax on a distaff: lay your yarn against some fiber, moisten the contact point, and pull out new fiber as you continue to spin.

SPINNING FLAX TOW

Hold the rolag lightly and overlap it with the leader.

Pull a length of unspun fiber from the tip of the rolag.

Let a bit of twist contact the end of the fiber and moisten the contact point.

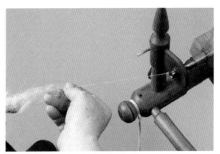

Slide your moistened dominant hand up the fiber, ahead of the twist.

USING ROLAGS ON A DISTAFF

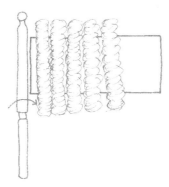

Lay rolags crosswise on a smooth ribbon or small towel.

Roll the piece in a bundle and tie it onto a straight shaft distaff.

Spinning Flax Sliver

Flax sliver has two forms: one that has an allover very short staple length and another that has a longer staple.

The first, called "cottonized" flax, has been reduced to a staple of about 1" (2.5 cm) and carded by a cotton-system machine. In this form, it spins with the same drafting zone length as cotton, but with a stiffness foreign to cotton.

Flax sliver is only 78 percent cellulose. Unlike cotton, it requires several launderings to become white. The spun yarn resembles the matte appearance and fuzziness of cotton. It has the content but few of the good qualities that would make you choose flax. Cottonized flax sliver is rarely available to handspinners.

The longer-stapled form of flax sliver ranges from 3" to 7" (7.5 to 18 cm) and is processed on wool-type carding and spinning systems. This kind of sliver can have a combed appearance, consistent staple length, and be considered "top." Or it can have a random, varied staple and be known as card sliver.

The top can have many of the valuable qualities of flax line: good luster, strength, and consistency. On the other hand, card sliver has those qualities to a lesser degree. Its varied staple length makes the yarn slubby and inconsistent, which reduces the fiber's inherent luster and, to some degree, its strength.

Many slivers are dyed luscious colors. Dyeing is a wet process and that alone can compress the sliver, making it difficult to draft. When pectin is still on the fiber, the compression is more persistent and some dye won't

Cottonized flax has a staple length of about 1" (2.5 cm).

Combed flax sliver *(top) has a consistent staple length;* ***card sliver*** *(bottom) has a random, varied staple.*

attach to the fiber as it should, making the sliver prone to crocking.[18]

Card sliver can sometimes benefit from being recarded, removing the neps and trash by hand, and then rolling it into rolags.

Spinning flax sliver requires a worsted draft, with the twist entirely ahead of your master hand.

---

[18] Crocking is a situation where dye is not attached to the fiber, but rather sits on the surface. Dye rubs off on your hands as you handle the fiber. Crocking is a symptom of a less-than-perfect dye process, often with no possible repair or resolution.

Tips for Spinning Flax Sliver

❦ Many elements help with your success in spinning flax sliver. The first is to draft and spin a fine yarn. As mentioned before, heavy flax yarns are difficult to keep consistent, whereas fine yarns give you time to smooth out the surface of the yarn and time to control the drafting zone.

❦ Spin sliver wet to help keep the surface of the yarn smooth and improve the luster. Because the flax fiber is stronger when wet, wet sliver can be spun into a very fine yarn. But remember to moisten just the point where the twist contacts the drafting zone; don't wet the entire rolag.

❦ Use a worsted draft—with twist only ahead of your lead, or dominant, hand—to improve the luster that's available in the fiber form.

❦ Set your wheel for a generous take-up, for even the carded material will produce a stiff yarn.

❦ Wind your spindle with a low angle.

❦ Treadle slowly at first—you can always pick up speed as you become more familiar with the fiber form.

❦ As with all machine-prepared materials, the sliver has a right end and a not-so-good end from which to spin. Try one end, break off, and try the other end. This should tell you which is which.

❦ Spin from the tip of the sliver and be careful not to crush the flax sliver, because it is easily compressed. Damp pressure is the worst.

❦ If you spin in moist conditions, such as humid summer or foggy days, take out only what you can spin in a short time. Don't leave flax sliver out in the open to be dampened and dried repeatedly. At least be aware that local conditions affect your fiber and its ability to draft freely.

Spinning Flax Sliver on a Wheel

Hold a short length of sliver in your non-dominant hand. Hold it lightly, keeping your thumb out of the drafting zone. Lay your yarn leader onto the sliver, making about a 7" (18 cm) overlap.

Moisten the tip of your dominant-hand fingers and place them where the leader contacts the sliver. Pull out a bit of unspun fiber with that hand and begin treadling slowly.

Slide your dominant hand up the leader and unspun fiber while slowly putting in twist.

Pull down some more fiber and slide your dominant hand up the leader and unspun fiber, moistening and smoothing the yarn as it's twisted, and allowing the yarn to be drawn onto the bobbin.

JOINING FLAX SLIVER ON A WHEEL

Hold the sliver very lightly in your nondominant hand and lay the the leader over the sliver for about 7" (18 cm).

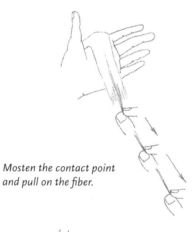

Mosten the contact point and pull on the fiber.

Slide your dominant hand up the leader and unspun fiber.

JOINING FLAX SLIVER ON A SPINDLE

Overlap the leader on the sliver.	*Pull down a length of fiber with your dominant hand.*	*Moisten the contact point and hold it while you set the spindle turning.*

Spinning Flax Sliver on a Spindle

If you're using a spindle, review the section on spinning line flax on a handspindle on page 82. Spinning line or sliver on a spindle has many similarities, except that instead of managing a distaff, you can hold the fiber in one hand. Sliver wound onto a wrist distaff would be practical, too, because there would be fewer joins.

To use a spindle, hold the sliver loosely in the palm of your nondominant hand.

To begin, lay the leader from your spindle on top of the sliver overlapping about 7" (18 cm).

Hold the fiber in the palm of your nondominant hand. Pinch the tip of the sliver and pull down a length of fiber with dominant hand.

Moisten the contact point with your dominant hand and hold that moistened contact point with your nondominant hand's thumb and forefinger while you set the spindle to turning (slowly at first).

  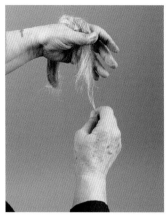

Pick up the contact point with your dominant hand and smooth and moisten the forming yarn.

Rotate your fiber hand to pinch the contact point while your dominant hand starts the spindle.

Pinch off the twist and pull down more fiber.

Pick up the contact point from your nondominant hand with your dominant hand and begin to smooth and moisten the forming yarn with your dominant hand.

To put more twist into the spindle, rotate the wrist of your nondominant hand so that its thumb and forefinger can pinch the yarn and keep the twist out of the sliver while, at the same time, your dominant hand adds twist to the spindle.

Bring your dominant hand close to the nondominant hand to pinch off the twist and pull more fiber from the sliver, then use your dominant hand to smooth and moisten the forming yarn, just ahead of the twist.

Frequently Asked Questions

Q. *I spin for a while and all goes well, then suddenly the fiber won't draft. What happened?*

A. The line fiber must flow freely. If it doesn't, check to see if the ribbon ends on the distaff have gotten tangled in the fiber. Or the ties may have slipped and are either too loose or too tight. If your distaff begins to look like a bad-hair day, then the fiber needs to be taken off and rehackled and the distaff redressed before you can press on spinning.

Q. *A lot of flax fiber accumulates around my spinning area. I tried cleaning it up with the vacuum, but it wrapped around the brushes and made a mess. What do I do?*

A. Carefully clip the long fibers away from the brushes in your vacuum, pull them free, and throw them away. Next time, use a straw broom to pick up the flax fiber bits before you vacuum.

Q. *I tried to tear off a piece of yarn and wow! It hurt my hand. Did I do something wrong?*

A. Don't attempt to break linen yarn with your hands. It's very strong and will likely cut you. Use scissors or a knife instead.

Q. *Normally, I leave a bit of yarn out the orifice of the flyer when I'm ready to quit. Is this a good way to leave my wheel?*

A. When you're through spinning for the day, let the yarn wind slowly onto the bobbin. Make sure that the last few inches or centimeters of the yarn are loosely wrapped and can be easily found. Avoid wrapping the yarn around a maiden or tension knob just in case someone else (two- or four-legged) treadles the wheel for you in your absence. Flax yarn, casually wrapped around flyer arms while the wheel is treadled, can find serious places to snag—and it's strong enough to endanger the integrity of your flyer.

CHAPTER THREE:

Hemp

Discussions of hemp, especially of **Cannabis sativa,** are often clouded with confusion and controversy. This is a pity. It's both a beautiful and useful fiber with long and illustrious history.

Well before the written word, hemp was used for nets, shelter, and clothing. Early Asian writings indicate that its stalk yielded fiber for yarns and that its seeds yielded oil. During the time of sailing ships and European exploration, hemp was crowned "King of Plant Fibers." The very word for sailcloth, "canvas," is derived from **Cannabis**. Hemp has been spun into a wide range of yarns, from rough, sturdy stuffs for canvas, cordage, and ropes to fine, lustrous yarns for sheer, transparent cloths.

Hemp Species

A COMMON CONFUSION LIES in the name because of the several fibers called hemp. Manila hemp (*Musa textilis*), Indian hemp (*Apocynum cannabinum*), sisal hemp (*Agave sisalana*), sunn hemp (*Crotalaria juncea*) and ambari hemp (*Hibiscus cannabinus*) have no relation to *Cannabis*. Many of these so-called hemp fibers aren't bast or stem fibers at all, but leaf fibers. Although these cordage fibers sometimes resemble hemp, they don't have the characteristic durability, rot resistance, and strength of true hemp.

Another point of confusion concerns the *Cannabis* species itself. Hemp is very adaptive. It grows tall when soils are rich and moist; it grows shorter and bushier in arid climes. Over the ages, humans have selected hemp plants to suit localized growing conditions and their need for fiber, medicine, and food. Taxonomists debate whether there are one, two, or even more true hemps.

It is *Cannabis indica*, a resinous, relatively short, multibranching hemp subspecies, that's known for its medicinal and psychoactive properties. Fiber hemp, *C. sativa*, is our focus. It's tall and lithe with few branches and contains little of the controversial chemistry of *C. indica*.

In the United States, legal controversy has put hemp fiber production in limbo. Although in some states it's legal to grow hemp, in all states it's illegal to do so without a federal permit. Hemp fiber, yarns, and fabrics are perfectly legal, however.

Hemp Fiber Characteristics

HEMP IS ABOUT 78 PERCENT CELLULOSE. The remaining components are waxes, oils, lignin, and ash. This composition means that as your finished hemp project is laundered, the yarns will release those oils, waxes, and some lignin, which will make the fibers whiter. The yarns likewise become finer by about 25 percent. Hemp has no pectin. Spinning hemp wet can help to increase the strength of a fine yarn, but it does nothing to control the hairiness of the yarn, as it does when you spin linen.

The cells that make up hemp fiber are stacked like bricks, which make the fiber strong. When hemp is wet, like many of its cellulose fiber cousins, it's stronger, more pliant, and less vulnerable to snapping under sudden pressure. Hemp permits rigorous laundering with little damage, making it superior for washcloths and towels. It's also resistant to rot and

*Cannabis indica (left) is a short multibranching plant whereas **fiber hemp** (C. sativa) is tall and lithe (right).*

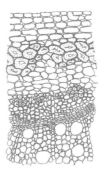

In cross-section, the cells of hemp fiber are stacked like bricks.

Hemp makes superior bags.

Hemp is nearly as strong as flax. Many variables play a role in natural fiber breaking strength: growing conditions, genetics, and relative fineness of the fiber. Rest assured that flax and hemp are extremely strong—to the point that they can readily cut your hand if you attempt to break them. Their ability to gag a vacuum is legendary.

Hemp is highly abrasion resistant. Like flax, it makes superior rug warps, bags, belting, canvas, cords, ropes, and other things that give hard service. It is as inelastic as wire.

Growing Hemp

'MOST HEMP IS DIOECIOUS, meaning it has male and female plants. The male plant is the fine fiber source. Fiber from the male plant is known as "fimble" hemp and can be as fine and white as flax. The female plant produces seed. Fiber can be harvested from the female plant, but it's coarse and of lower quality. The two crops mature at different times. Male fiber plants reach maturity weeks before the female plants produce ripe seeds. Therefore, when grown primarily for fiber, the crop is harvested before seeds mature and yields few, if any, seeds. When grown for seed, the male plants are well past their prime and the quality of the fiber is much diminished.

It's tempting to compare the habit and growth of hemp and flax. Like flax, hemp has spinnable fibers ringing the stem just beneath the plant's bark. These phloem cells transfer food between the leaves and roots of the plant. Unlike flax, hemp has a second layer of very fine fibers between the phloem cells and the core. The interior of the stem has pith and a hollow core. Also unlike flax, the hemp fiber has a scattering of long, slender cells filled with a brownish-red material that give hemp its natural beige tint.

salt-water damage. Hemp gained its reputation as King of the Plant Fibers because hemp ropes and canvas for sailing ships outlasted any other material of its time.

Hemp is both absorbent and cool to the touch. This combination makes hemp attractive for summertime apparel, whether knitted, crocheted, or woven. The bonus is it dries quickly. What could be more comfortable?

Strong alkalis do not harm hemp, but mild acids will destroy it. Thus, you can wash hemp in lye soaps or place it in contact with alkali soils or water, and the fibers won't be damaged. More likely, the yarns will become lighter in color and more lustrous. But drop a spot of tomato on your hemp placemat or dribble a soda on your shirt, and you'll want to rinse the spot to prevent its turning into a hole. As that spot dries, the acids will become more concentrated, acidic, and destructive.

The hemp stalk, unlike that of flax, is robust—often several inches (several centimeters) in diameter rather than millimeters. The core can also be hollow. Whereas flax thrives in a cool, damp climate, hemp is remarkably adaptive. It can produce fiber in a variety of soils and environments. When it's grown in moist, rich soils and temperate climates, hemp can produce a mature fiber-bearing stalk 15 feet (4.5 m) tall in 120 days. In less-than-optimal soils and growing conditions, the plant still attains a height of 5 to 8 feet (1.5 to 2.5 m). In comparison, superior flax thrives in cool climates and grows to 40" (101.5 cm) tall.

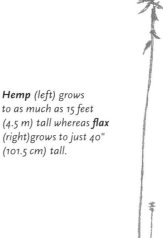

Hemp (left) grows to as much as 15 feet (4.5 m) tall whereas *flax* (right) grows to just 40" (101.5 cm) tall.

Harvesting Hemp

WHEN IT COMES TO HARVESTING, hemp and flax have much in common. In some areas of the world, hemp is retted—the hemp fiber is cut close to the ground and bundled to dry. When dry, the de-seeded bundles are placed in a pond or tank to ret, or they are laid out in the field to dew-ret. The retting progress is checked regularly and, when judged complete, the pond-retted bundles are rinsed and again laid out to dry. Dew-retted hemp is simply gathered. Complicated by hemp's natural resistance to rot and the stalks' robust size, the retting process for hemp takes more time than that for flax.

After retting, the hemp is "broken," meaning the pithy core is crushed. The bark and bits of broken core, known as hurds or "boon," are scutched in a manner similar to flax. Hackling completes the removal of off-grade short fibers and makes the remaining fiber parallel. Hemp in this form is also called "line."

Another common method of harvesting, called "decortication," scrapes the fiber from the stem. Decortication is performed on green (freshly harvested) or partially retted hemp. This process doesn't preserve the full length of the fiber, as retting does, to produce hemp line. Instead, these shorter fibers are processed into sliver.

Whether short or long, line or sliver, hemp makes useful, hardwearing, yet beautiful, yarns. Considering that it has clothed, housed, and carried us many long miles, hemp is truly a tie to our past. Let's spin some.

Spinning Hemp

AT THIS POINT, if you've been with me from the start, you should have a good idea of the practical aspects of spinning cotton and flax. With hemp, you can rest on your laurels a bit. You should be acquainted with and comfortable holding cotton fiber with a light touch. You're also familiar with the necessary adjustments to make on your wheel to take care of a wiry flax yarn. More importantly, you're aware of the twist and where it is as you spin. Spinning hemp should be a piece of cake!

As you begin to spin hemp yarn, you'll find yourself using techniques common to the making of both cotton and flax yarns. Hemp sliver has both the compressibility of cotton (if you squash it, it won't spin) and a staple length and stiffness similar to flax.

If you've jumped right to hemp, bypassing earlier chapters, don't despair. I'll review the essentials of hemp spinning before moving into the step-by-step processes.

You can currently buy two forms of hemp: line and sliver. Line is the full-length combed (hackled) hemp fiber. Hemp line can be as

Don't squash hemp fiber with your thumb.

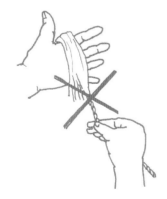

Never let the twist past your wheel-side hand.

much as 5 to 7 feet (1.5 to 2.1 m) long. Sliver is a soft "rope" of carded hemp with an average staple length of 3" to 5" (7.5 to 12.5 cm). The rope typically ranges from about the diameter of a broomstick to that of your wrist. The two fiber forms—line and sliver—are handled very differently and the yarns they produce are likewise strikingly dissimilar.

Spinning Line Hemp

Line hemp is a pretty rare commodity. It has to come from hemp that has been submitted to a sequence of processes: retting, drying, breaking, scutching, and hackling. If you're fortunate and have some, treat it like line flax. Hackle it and dress a distaff as described on page 73— it will be longer than you can manage just by holding onto it. Because hemp has no pectin to glue it to itself, the fiber on your distaff will survive changes in humidity much better than flax. You can therefore be more casual with the volume of material on the distaff.

Spinning line hemp is so similar to spinning line flax (see page 78) that to repeat the instructions here would be redundant. But a quick review of key points is in order.

- ❧ Dress the line flax onto a distaff.

- ❧ Draft with two hands.

- ❧ Set your wheel adjustments for moderate take-up.

- ❧ Never let the twist run past your two hands and up into the fiber on the distaff. Truth is, you should never let the twist get past your wheel-side hand; this is true worsted spinning.

- ❧ Change hooks frequently.

- ❧ Spinning hemp wet will aid in strengthening your fine yarn, but it won't smooth down the fuzzies.

Ultrafine Japanese hemp yarns are extraordinary.

Carded silver is the most readily available form of hemp fiber.

Do spin hemp line into a fine yarn. How fine? Aim for yarn about the size of the wire in a paper clip. When you're comfortable spinning that, spin the size of dental floss. If you need a larger finished yarn, then ply it. Heavy hemp singles are perfect for making burlap. If you're after something softer, smoother, and better—well, remember the silk purse.

If you have hemp in line form, you possess a precious luxury fiber. Line hemp is the source for ultrafine clothing yarns. When it's spun as such a yarn, it softens in time to something virtually indistinguishable from the choicest heirloom linen.

Spinning Hemp Sliver

The most readily available form of hemp fiber is carded sliver. Rather than processing the hemp stalk by retting, this material is frequently decorticated, or scraped from green stalks. The scraped fiber has a multitude of staple lengths and a pretty broad range of fiber diameters from coarse to fine. Like all machine-prepared fibers, the sliver itself will have a "nap," which means it will spin more easily from one end than the other. Spinning from the "wrong" end of the sliver will result in uncontrolled slubs, a hairy surface, and rough and erratic drafting characteristics. Spinning from the "good" end will produce a smooth, more consistent yarn with greater ease.

Tow hemp on handheld distaff.

Carded materials have an assortment of different staple lengths, which causes slubs. If the differences in length are minor, there will be fewer or longer slubs. An extreme variety of lengths is a recipe for "pom-poms-on-a-thread" style of novelty yarn. The truth is, the best way to spin smooth, even yarn (if you don't have line flax) is to spin from the most consistent source—top or combed sliver—from which all the short bits have been removed. Nothing prevents you from hackling the carded sliver and sorting the staple lengths (see page 69). Then you can dress it on a distaff, as you would tow flax (see page 86).

If your fiber has been dyed in the sliver, the wet process will have certainly condensed it. Hemp isn't elastic and won't spring back like a wool rolag. You can't tease it open as you would flax. If you have a sliver that simply won't draft as you would like, you might want to reprocess it—card it into rolags or hackle it and sort the staples. Although reprocessing would seem to add a lot of time added to your project, it will actually put yarn in your hands a lot faster. And, it will be a better, smoother, and more consistent yarn, too. If, on the other hand, you think you'll miss all the finicky, stop/start progress of trying to coax and cajole that sliver that looked so good in the bag but then turned ugly at the wheel or spindle, then by all means, don't reprocess the fiber.

A handheld distaff works well for tow hemp.

Spinning Hemp Sliver on a Wheel

The first steps are to lubricate and adjust your wheel. Oil your wheel according to the manufacturer's suggestions—general oiling points are given on page 31. Because hemp, like flax, is wiry and you'll want to build a firm yarn package on the bobbin, adjust your wheel for a moderate take-up. If the yarn package is too loose on the bobbin, the individual mounds of yarn will fall over and open up and allow the next layer of yarn to cut into them. (Believe me, this situation makes unwinding truly nerve-wracking.)

The design of the **single-drive bobbin-lead wheel** will most likely give you enough take-up to get started on an empty bobbin. Just oil up your wheel, and you're ready to go. As the bobbin fills, complex physics will cause the wind-on characteristics to change. At this point, you may need to increase the take-up by increasing the tension on the flyer brake band. Note that small increases in flyer brake-band tension can cause big changes in the take-up. Go easy.

For a **single-drive flyer-lead wheel**, you'll want to slightly increase the tension on the bobbin brake band. You may also need to lightly increase the drive cord tension. These two adjustments are interrelated on the scotch tension wheel. Keep in mind that you should still be able to treadle your wheel without much effort. However, as the bobbin fills, it will become heavier and take more effort to stall. If this happens, you'll want to increase the tension on the bobbin brake. If any of these changes increases your treadling effort dramatically, then stop. Nobody wants to pump hard. You have options. If you change the original plastic brake band to a slightly larger cotton yarn, you'll be able to adjust those tensions with greater sensitivity and less treadling effort.

For a **double-drive wheel**, use flyer and bobbin whorls of very different diameters, making sure that the bobbin whorl is the smaller one. Exactly which flyer whorl and which bobbin whorl to use is something you'll have to sort out while spinning. You can probably use the same set up you used for spinning line flax to

---

WAYS TO INCREASE TAKE-UP

Increase tension on the flyer brake band of a single-drive bobbin-lead wheel.

Increase tension on the bobbin brake band of a single-drive flyer-lead wheel.

Use a larger flyer whorl with a small bobbin whorl on a double-drive wheel.

spin hemp sliver, especially if the yarns are similar in size.

Compared to cotton and flax, hemp sliver is the most "wool-like" of the plant fibers. It has some "tack" like wool, so it drafts with a more familiar resistance. The staple length of hemp sliver is also similar to that of wool.

Be aware that hemp will compress like cotton. You won't be able to get away with the type of casual or rough handling that you can with wool. Perhaps it won't compress as readily as cotton, but once condensed, hemp is mired, sodden, and unresponsive until recarded. You can't tease it open. Shaking or snapping the sliver sometimes works if the sliver hasn't become too dense. But it's best to nurture the habit of holding the sliver lightly. Resist the temptation to put your fiber hand thumb down on it (i.e., don't crush the "hooey" out of it).

Hemp, like cotton, will draft with less twist than you think you'll need. If you let too much twist into the sliver, the yarn will turn into a gross, monstrous thing and drafting will stop dead. You can pull but nothing will happen—everything is "locked." When this occurs, pull out the gross bit, throw it away, and join on again. Once the twist gets buried into the sliver in this way, the twist has already squeezed the fiber past the point of being draftable.

Join onto your leader and begin to treadle slowly, then use a worsted draft as follows:

Begin with your wheel-side hand at the point where the twist contacts the drafting zone.

Move your wheel-side hand toward the wheel, then draft more fiber.

Follow the twist up the forming yarn.

Use your fiber-side hand as a distaff to support the hemp sliver.

DRAFTING HEMP SLIVER

If the twist gets buried in the sliver, the fiber cannot be drafted.

Use your fiber hand as a distaff to support the hemp sliver.

Move your wheel hand to pull out more fiber.

Begin with your wheel hand on the contact point between the yarn and fiber.

Slide your wheel hand up the fiber, always staying ahead of the twist.

Spinning hemp progresses with a rhythmic repeat of pulling out with the wheel-side hand, sliding up the forming yarn (never opening the thumb and forefinger of that hand), and pulling out more fiber with the wheel-side hand as you wind the spun yarn onto the bobbin. Whether you pull out with the wheel hand or pull back with the fiber hand is a matter of personal preference; the result is the same. But the key is to not let the twist get behind your wheel-side hand—it should never get between your hands.

Spin off the end or the tip of the sliver. If the sliver is too large to manage comfortably, don't predraft it. If you over-handle it, as might happen with predrafting, you're likely to compress it and it won't draft at all. It's far better to break the sliver into 8" (20.5 cm) lengths, then split those in half lengthwise.

If the sliver just isn't working for you, load some fiber onto a single handcard with a lashing motion, then spin off the handcard as if it were a distaff of sorts, as shown in the box at right.

Spinning from a Handcard

Break off an 8" (20.5 cm) length of sliver. Holding the handcard wire side up with the handle pointing away from you, pass the tip of the sliver across the card, beginning at the handle and ending at the opposite edge. In effect, you want to "wipe" the fiber into the clothing of the card. This will leave a sheer stripe of fiber along the face of the card, from handle to edge.

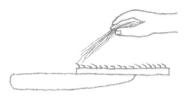

Pass sliver across card.

Move your hand down the sliver a bit, then make another wipe on top of the same stripe. In this way, load the handcard with shorter lengths of opened fiber.

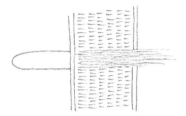

Make another wipe.

Spin from the "beard" of fiber that hangs off the edge of the card opposite the handle.

beard with a downward angle.

A final solution is to break off staple lengths of fiber and recard them into rolags, as described for dressing tow rolags on a distaff on page 75.

Spin off the card as it it were a distaff.

Tips for Spinning Hemp

❀ Spin a fine yarn (think "thread" more than "yarn"). Hemp is very strong, and it makes a strong, fine yarn. Like flax, when spun coarsely, it will quickly resemble twisted paper, rope, or burlap.

Large bast singles resemble twisted paper, rope, or burlap.

❀ Hemp is stronger when wet, but because it has no pectin, it won't spin smooth with moisture. Still, you may find that wetting it helps when you're spinning a fine yarn.

❀ To spin a fine yarn, the drafting zone should be sheer enough to see through. Therefore, you'll generally want to draft back or pull out faster than you normally would for robust yarns.

❀ Change hooks on the flyer frequently to prevent great "mountains" from forming on the bobbin. The wiry hemp yarn will slide down the mountains to disastrous result. The care you take when you wind onto the bobbin will pay off when you unwind it.

❀ Don't try to break the yarn between your hands. Use scissors.

❀ Spin a consistent-sized yarn, spreading the twist evenly along it. As you spin hemp (or flax), if your yarn breaks, leaving a blunt end that looks scissorcut, it means that so much twist accumulated in a fine section of yarn it actually ruptured the yarn.

The yarn will break if too much twist is added to a small section.

Spinning Hemp Sliver on a Handspindle

With attention to a few details, hemp sliver can be easily managed on a handspindle.

Given that hemp is stiffer than most wools (and is, in fact, more similar to mohair and other hair fibers), you'll want a spindle with plenty of weight to overcome the inherent stiffness. Because hemp is also very strong, you'll be able to spin fine yarn even with a surprisingly heavy spindle.

Pick a spindle with a robust shaft—more than ¼" (6 mm) in diameter—unless your goal is sewing thread. The larger the shaft, the more slowly the spindle puts in the twist, which is good for a beginner. Both high-whorl and low-whorl spindles have their uses and advocates. Start with the style that's most comfortable for you.

Go ahead and spin a fine yarn. Fine yarns take more twist, which gives you time to manage the spindle while you draft, and you'll end up with a yarn that's useful either as a singles or plied yarn. Save the heavier yarns for when you become more comfortable with spindle-spinning hemp. (Heavy bast yarns, which are very dependent on careful fiber preparation, are not easy to spin.)

Start out by spinning slowly. Hemp has a long staple, is stiff, and doesn't require as much twist as a fine, soft wool yarn. You can speed up when you become accustomed to the fiber.

Wind firmly onto the spindle, forming a spread-mesh pattern by turning the spindle while making a rapid move from one side of the copp to the other. Doing so lays the yarn at a low angle to the spindle shaft and builds a yarn package that's pointed at each end with a plump tummy in the middle. It manages wiry fine yarn and permits you to unwind the spindle from the side under tension. The following chapters discuss unwinding yarns further.

Use a worsted draft so that the twist is always between the spindle and your lead hand. Draft between your fiber and lead hands and take care to never pinch the drafting zone with your fiber hand—always pinch the yarn below the drafting zone.

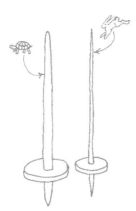

The larger the spindle shaft, the slower the spindle will add twist.

Spin a fine yarn about the diameter of a paper clip.

Wind the yarn firmly onto the spindle at a low angle.

Join hemp to the leader much the same as you would join flax.

To begin, break off a short length of sliver slightly longer than the staple length and hold it lightly in your nondominant hand.

Lay the leader from your spindle on top of the sliver and rotate the spindle in your fingers until the leader contacts and begins to grab fibers in the sliver.

Pinch the point where the fibers are gathering around the leader with your nondominant hand.

Rotate the spindle with your dominant hand, then use the same hand to pinch the point where the fibers gather around the leader while holding the fiber lightly with your nondominant hand.

Draft some fiber with your dominant hand, then slide that hand up the forming yarn. The fiber will be joined to your spindle and you're set up to spin hemp worsted-style on a suspended spindle!

As you spin, your nondominant hand will act as a distaff for the tuft of hemp, plus temporarily take over for your dominant hand when the latter is twirling the spindle. Your dominant hand will draft the fiber, control the twist as it enters the drafting zone (remember: no twist between your hands), *and* keep the spindle turning. If someone asks "What time is it?" offer up a cheesy grin.

You can dress a distaff with sliver and spin more yarn with fewer joins, as described in Chapter 2.

SPINDLE SPINNING AT A GLANCE

Join on, pinch with your fiber hand, and rotate the spindle.

Pinch with your spindle hand and draft with your fiber hand.

Follow the twist with your spindle hand.

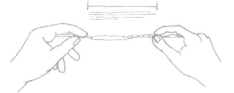

With your hands a staple length apart, untwist the slub.

Pull the yarn apart.

Lay the end of the yarn on the fiber mass, add twist, and pull the yarn.

Making Joins

When the twist gets away from you, pull the resulting giant slub out of the sliver, then go back to a thinner section of yarn.

Hold your hands a staple length apart, using the longest staple length in your sliver.

Untwist the yarn until the fibers are parallel once again.

Pull the fibers apart in the end of the yarn to produce a feathered end instead of a tightly twisted tail. This open, brush-like end can then be laid on the sliver.

Rotate the spindle without drafting.

When the fibers in the sliver begin to contact and adhere to the end of the yarn, continue to rotate the spindle with your fingers and begin to pull on the end of the yarn. Doing so transfers the twist to the drafting zone and drafts the end of your yarn to the attached sliver.

Voilà! Your join has been made. Joins such as this take practice to perfect, but are worth the effort because they can be seamless, smooth, and strong enough to use as a singles warp yarn.

A Few Words on Slubs

Slubs are another issue. There are two kinds of slubs.[19] One type forms gradual swellings and thinnings that extend along several inches (several centimeters) because of the variety of staple lengths in the fiber. This type of slub comes with the territory and will affect the smoothness of your final knitted or woven piece—and lends a charming "handspun" quality to the piece.

The second kind of slub, called an uncontrolled slub, is a red flag. This type of large and "spontaneous" (read: uncontrolled) slub will affect your yarn's durability. Let's take a look at what makes this so.

When spinning, twist runs to the fine areas of your yarn, collects there, and makes those lengths strong. Where there are slubs, there is less fiber-to-fiber contact and less twist to hold in the fibers. Because the slub "sticks up" out of the knitted or woven structure, it is more vulnerable to abrasion, especially along cuffs, necklines, hems, corners, and selvedges.

Slubs that are longer than the fiber staple length will compromise the integrity of your yarn. There won't be enough twist to keep the slub fibers in the yarn and the yarn will abrade. You can pull chunks of these loose fibers from the structure, leaving thin spots. The twist in the adjacent yarn will transfer to the thin spots and the entire softly spun area will become vulnerable. This is the point at which a yarn will fail—just like nature abhors a vacuum, twist runs to the point of least resistance.

If you see gross, uncontrolled slubs, stop and figure out what's causing them. If the fiber

Gradual slubs lend a charming "handspun" quality to yarn.

Uncontrolled slubs will affect a yarn's durability.

Slubs that are longer than the fiber's staple length will eventually pull apart.

isn't flowing freely, think about how you can get it to flow. Is your thumb on the drafting zone making a nice wadded quid beneath it that just won't draft? Does the fiber need to be recarded? Are you treadling at a constant rate or are you slowing down to manage some problem? What problem? Yarn generally comes out pretty well when you can spin without much thought. If you play Spinners' Whac-A-Mole while you spin, your yarn will show it. Slow down. Relax. Use good materials. Don't mess with them.

---

19 In past times, slubs were called "twits." It still fits.

Frequently Asked Questions

Q. *My yarn spins at a fine gauge for a while, then suddenly it gets large. What am I doing?*

A. It only takes a moment of inattention for twist to get past your lead hand and into the fiber supply. Because hemp, like all soft plant fibers, is easily compressed, it won't draft after the twist has plunged headlong into the mass. To control the size of a hemp yarn, you need to constantly be aware of how much twist is between your lead hand and the fiber supply. What you need is none.

Q. *Does hemp get as white as flax does after it's laundered a lot?*

A. Bast fibers "whiten," but each fiber has its own "white." Ramie is snow; flax, milk; and hemp, a soft pearl. If you want to pursue the possibilities of white-on-white color work, sample and launder the yarns and see if the result pleases.

Q. *Is it possible to smoke hemp fiber and get high?*

A. No (unless we're talking about the high you can get from holding your breath).

In previous chapters, you've spun soft cotton yarns on spindle, charkha, and treadled wheel. You have seen flax processed from straw to lustrous line, perhaps dreaming of finely carved distaves of many kinds that will help you spin smooth, lustrous flax and hemp yarns. Your twinkling spindles bulge and your wheel bobbins can take no more. Thus concludes our lesson on the making of yarn. Soon we must speak of other matters. What happens next?

CHAPTER FOUR:

Yarn Handling

When you first spin a new fiber, you'll need all your concentration. However, after you've filled several bobbins, you'll relax. You'll casually reach for a fresh bobbin and realize that you have filled them all. Now what? This brings us to the next step—transferring the yarn from your bobbin or spindle onto another bobbin or into a skein or ball. Unless you have the proper setup, yarn handling can occupy a great deal of time. For this reason, we're going to sit down, push the wheel aside, and talk about the advantages, techniques, and efficiencies of yarn handling.

First, you'll have a chance to check the yarn for irregularities. You can do this while winding briskly—the slubs and lightly twisted areas are easy to spot. It's a good idea to repair or remove the off-grade sections before you ply. Doing so gives you the option of running the bobbins of yarn back through the wheel to modify the twist where needed—a significant benefit if you've used costly fiber or plan on large project. It's better to know sooner than later if you have an off-grade skein—at least you have a chance to rework or replace it.

Second, if you rewind your yarn a couple of yards (meters) from your wheel or bobbin (called cross-reeling), the twist will even out over that distance, making a much more consistent, better yarn. In other words, simply reeling it across the room will improve your yarn.

Actually, it's a good idea to leave the same bobbin in your wheel for an entire project, continuing to fill and unwind it. Although your bobbins appear to be identical, they don't behave so. Spinning on the same bobbin helps to keep your project yarn more consistent.

Unwinding your bobbins and spindles has other benefits as well. Freshly spun yarns are lively things. They kink back on themselves when given the least opportunity. If your cotton singles have enough twist to make a good warp yarn, they'll certainly curl back on themselves and tangle. Linen and hemp yarns are often more stiff than kinky. Think about what you need to do next.

These yarns may need to be plied, made up into a warp, or knitted from a ball. The prospect of trying to herd these unwilling characters is enough to make you consider waxing the kitchen floor or re-alphabetizing your CD collection instead. Take heart. These unset yarns are in a transitory state. A hot-water treatment will tame them by "setting the twist." Once the

Wind the yarn from your bobbin onto a stainless or plastic cone or cylinder for setting the twist.

twist is set, the stiffness and kinks are either reduced or gone entirely. Cotton yarns become limp and soft; linen and hemp yarns become pliant and supple. (Music swells.)

Besides setting the twist, hot water and soap will wash out field contamination, plant waxes, oils, and pectin. Your yarn becomes cleaner and whiter, as well as more manageable. It will dye better after a good soapy boil, too.

After you've spun yards of fine yarn, you'll need to get it off your bobbin and into the suds. It's too bad you can't just plop the bobbin into the water. Even if it's plastic, however, this approach has hazards. Many plastics soften and lose their shape at temperatures well below the boiling point. Before you submit your spun yarn to a boiling scour, test your bobbins or cones in hot, soapy water. Or resort to stainless-steel or dye-house cast offs. Your spinning bobbins need to be concentric and balanced. If they become deformed, their erratic behavior when you spin will let you know it.

114

A niddy-noddy is a type of skein winder.

An umbrella swift is a type of skein unwinder.

To set the twist, plant fibers need to simmer for 20 to 60 minutes. You can put skeins of linen or hemp yarn directly in a pot to boil. But it's best to keep cotton yarns under tension because any "pig tails" set into them will become failure points when tension is placed on the straightened yarn.

Commercial dye houses use cylindrical or conical yarn cores that are permeated with holes. They're great for boiling cotton—simply use a bobbin winder to wind the yarn onto them. The recipe and procedure for scouring and setting twist follow the general yarn-handling techniques outlined below.

General Yarn-Handling Techniques

Consider the tools and methods that make yarn handling quick and relatively painless.[20] Tools that organize and store yarn should be classed in pairs—a skein winder and a skein unwinder. For example, a niddy-noddy is a skein winder. You can't get the skein back onto the niddy to unwind it—you'll need an umbrella swift for that purpose. Reels are winders; swifts are unwinders.

---

20 Yarn handling goes better with reasonable tools. After 35-some years weaving, knitting, and spinning, I would gladly limit myself to a single wheel so that I would have efficient winding gear.

Another yarn form or "package" is the cone. Yarn is wound onto a cone with the help of a bobbin winder. The cone is an efficient winding/unwinding form because to unwind it, you can put it on the floor and wind from the end. The cone then becomes the unwinder. The center-pull ball works the same way.

When you wind yarn from your wheel onto a storage bobbin, you'll use a bobbin winder. Your lazy kate is the unwinder.

You can unwind yarn from a cone of yarn or a center-pull ball.

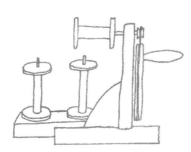

Use a bobbin winder to wind yarn from your wheel onto a storage bobbin. Use a lazy kate to unwind yarn from the storage bobbin(s).

Unwinding from a Bobbin onto Another Bobbin

You can leave the bobbin in the wheel when winding it off. Either slip the drive cord off the bobbin or release the tension on the brake. For a double-drive setup, put both loops on the flyer whorl and increase tension on the drive cord to snub the flyer. Position the flyer arms so that they stay out of the way while reeling.

Alternatively, you can dismount the flyer/bobbin and put the bobbin on your lazy kate. Position your bobbin winder so that you'll pull the yarn off at right angles to the bobbin shaft.

Place the two bobbins as far apart as possible while transferring to help even out the twist.

Put a dab of oil on the unwinding bobbin bearings. They run more sweetly with oil.

Put an empty bobbin on the winder.

Be careful to lay the yarn on the bobbin in gradual, even layers. Don't wind knobs next to one another, as can happen when you spin. At this point, there should be minimal hills and

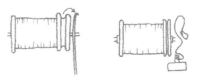

Slip the cord off the bobbin or release the brake.

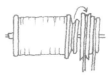

For a double-drive setup, put both loops on the flyer whorl.

valleys, which will let you unwind this bobbin at an even speed.

Speaking of speed: be aware that the bobbin you're winding onto is rotating at a pretty constant speed. The bobbin in your wheel will speed up and slow down as the yarn moves across the hills and into the valleys. As your wheel bobbin empties, its circumference is gradually reduced, which makes it turn faster. To make the situation more complex, the bobbin you're filling increases its circumference. Rather than devolve into a discussion of changing speeds as you wind, just place the winding setup so that you're in a position to watch the wheel bobbin as you unwind it. That way, you can be responsive to the changing rate of yarn coming off of it.

TIPS FOR UNWINDING BOBBINS

Lay the yarn on the bobbin in gradual, even layers.

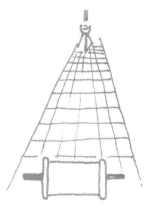

Place the two bobbins as far apart as possible.

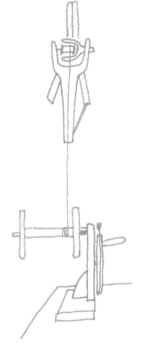

Position the bobbin winder so that the yarn pulls off perpendicular to the bobbin shaft.

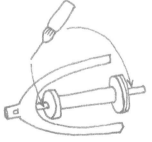

Oil the bobbin bearings so they'll run smoothly.

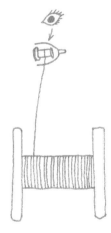

Keep an eye on the wheel bobbin as it unwinds.

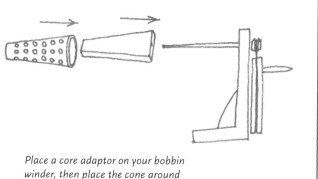

Place a core adaptor on your bobbin winder, then place the cone around the adaptor.

Wind firm, sheer layers at a low angle so that the yarn makes x's across the cone.

Unwinding from a Bobbin onto a Cone

Use the same setup as described for unwinding from a bobbin to another bobbin, working either from your wheel or lazy kate.

Place a core adaptor on your bobbin winder, then the cone.

Overlap a couple of winds to secure the yarn to the cone, then begin to lay an even layer—just one yarn thick—over the "holey" part of the cone. (The boiling water can't reach the yarn on the cone where there are no holes.) Continue to wind firm, sheer layers of yarn. The yarn should not lay "shoulder to shoulder" with the yarn next to it, but spaced at a lower angle so that the yarn makes ×'s across the cone and layers beneath.

Stop when the thickness of the yarn laid on the cone is about ¼" (6 mm) thick. Just pat the end of the yarn against the cone. Cotton is "sticky" and will adhere to itself.

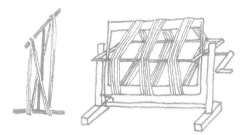

A **niddy-noddy** (left) is useful for winding small amounts of yarn, but a **reel** (right) is more efficient if you're dealing with hundreds of yards.

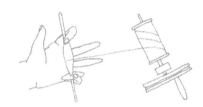

Use a light touch if you hold the spindle in your hand while winding onto a bobbin.

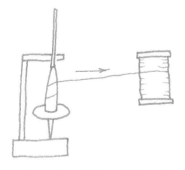

Alternatively, rest the spindle on its tip and support the shaft with your hand or makeshift stand.

Unwinding From a Bobbin into a Skein

Set up as above, either from your wheel or lazy kate. Don't forget the dab of oil on the bobbin bearings. You can wind onto a niddy-noddy or a reel. Clock reels and blocking reels by far out-perform a niddy-noddy. The chief advantages of the niddy are its compact footprint and economy. For handling hundreds of yards of fine yarn, it rapidly becomes a trial.[21]

Winding from a Handspindle onto a Bobbin

If you want to ply the singles spun on your handspindle, then, realistically, the best way to ply them is on the wheel. This gives you the possibility of working these very fine yarns with reasonable control.[22]

Although it's possible to hold your full spindle in one hand while winding the yarn onto the bobbin, you'll need a light touch and sensitivity to the changing behavior of the spindle. It helps if the yarn is reasonably strong, too. Otherwise, set up your spindle to rest on its tip and support the shaft with either one hand or a makeshift stand.

These methods take the yarn from the side of the spindle, not over the end. Each spindle is different, but with some thought and an adventurous nature (and a trip to the hardware store), you can engineer a lazy kate for most spindles.

---

21 I think of a Gary Larson-esque cartoon, one frame with a devil saying "Welcome to Hell" while he hands the newbie a niddy, while in the next frame the angel says, "Welcome to Heaven" and gives the newbie a blocking reel.

22 You may find that some of your singles need to be set before you ply them. In this case, wind them off into a skein if they're bast fibers or onto a cone if they're cotton. You can ply the set, dried cotton directly from the cones.

Winding from a Handspindle onto a Cone

If you've spun the yarn on a small spindle, you'll want to wind the yarn onto a cone. For cotton, the cone you used to boil the yarn is the best tool. So set up your bobbin winder with a core adaptor and cone. With a little practice, you can lightly hold your spindle in one hand and wind with the other.

Winding this way works for a side-delivery situation. If your spindle has been wound for end-feed, then just hold one end of the spindle and wind off the other tip.

The tahkli has a hook with a sharp end point on one end and a sharp point on the other. Traditionally, the tahkli would be placed between a split reed and unwound from there. If your tahkli is a nontraditional form, you can manage with one end in a smooth bowl and the index and thumb of one hand encircling the top of the spindle while the other hand runs the bobbin winder.

WINDING FROM A SMALL HANDSPINDLE ONTO A CONE

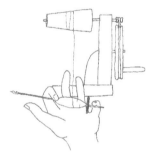

For side delivery, lightly hold the spindle in one hand and wind with the other.

For end-feed delivery, hold one end of the spindle and wind off the other tip.

Wedge a traditional tahkli between a split reed.

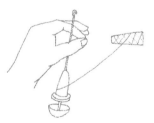

Rest a nontraditional tahkli in a smooth bowl and encircle the top with you thumb and index finger.

Winding from a Handspindle into a Skein

Most likely you'll be winding a bast fiber skein from a larger spindle. If you're using a niddy-noddy, you can hold your spindle lightly so it will unwind as you traverse the niddy-noddy. Winding a skein on a reel is similar, only it goes much faster. Hold the spindle lightly while turning the reel.

WINDING FROM A HANDSPINDLE INTO A SKEIN

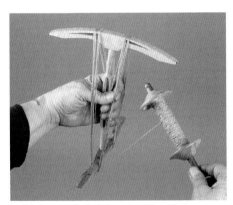

Hold the spindle lightly so it will unwind as you traverse the niddy-noddy.

Hold the spindle lightly while turning the reel.

Winding from a Charkha onto a Bobbin or Cone

If you've spun your cotton on the charkha and you want to ply it, you'll need to transfer it to bobbins. Let's assume that you've determined that the yarn doesn't need to be set before it's plied. To ply, you'll need to have the bobbins on your lazy kate.

In this situation, it's important to build the cop on your spindle carefully with an eye to unwinding the spindle from the tip, not the side, so the spindle doesn't need to turn to dispense the yarn. What you need is a cone-shaped package on your spindle.

Set your charkha so that the yarn comes directly off the tip of the spindle, which is pointing at your bobbin on the bobbin winder: a straight line of sight. Any deflection from this straight line from the axis of the spindle to the bobbin may result in time spent straightening out tangled yarn, broken yarn, tears, and a dire need for chocolate.

WINDING FROM A CHARKHA

Build the cop in a cone-shaped package that will unwind from the tip.

Wind onto the bobbin in a straight line from the axis of the spindle.

Wind the cones and bobbins as previously mentioned: for bobbins, wind smooth, even layers; for the cone, wind with rapid traverse, making yarn x's on the cone.

If your charkha spindle is wound for side delivery, then it must turn to dispense the yarn. That means that you'll take the spindle out of the charkha bearings and hold it lightly in your hand, or set it into its own lazy kate.

The charkha spindle often has points on each end. Like the tahkli, it can be set in a split piece of cane held in your hand, which acts as a lazy kate. Wind slowly at first until you have a sense of the system and how to run it. Then you can speed up.

General Tips for Winding Yarn

As the yarn passes through your hands, check it for soundness and consistency. Remove any off-grade lengths. Tie knots with long tails, so they're obvious when you use the yarn. You'll have fewer unpleasant surprises when you convert your yarn into a finished item.

Although cotton sticks to itself and rarely needs more than a pat to secure the end to a bobbin or cone, hemp and flax are quite different. They will readily slither off, rapidly falling to disarray. Tie the end of the yarn to a previous wrap.

Winding Skeins

First, tie the end of the skein to the beginning—you'll want to find this later. Tie your skeins in at least three places with figure-eight ties. If the yarn is fine, or has high twist, increase the number of ties (you really can't have too many). The ties help prevent the skein from snagging

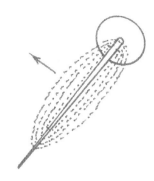

Spindle wound for side delivery.

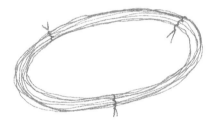

Tie skeins with figure-eight ties to prevent them from snagging and becoming disarranged.

and becoming disarranged. After you've spent long minutes trying to reconstruct a tangled skein, you'll think better of the short time it takes to add a few more ties.

If you anticipate dyeing your skeins, tie them loosely so there won't be a color mark at the tie.

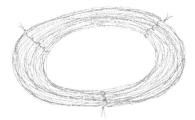

Don't wind enormous skeins of fine yarn.

Skeins can tangle in boiling water. This is why skeins are not the recommended form for setting fine, lively cotton yarns. Skeins are much better for hemp and linen yarns.

Make a good match between the fineness of your yarn and the diameter and bulk of your skein. Have you ever tried to unwind a one- or two-pound (0.5 to 1 kg) skein of fine yarn? The weight of the skein is the challenge. Your good winding buddies' arms get tired after the first hour or so.

An umbrella swift won't turn easily if it's holding such a heavy skein. Other swifts will manage the weight, but if required to turn to dispense the yarn, the weight of the skein is

often enough to break the yarn. Another factor is the diameter of your skein. Fine yarns do not unreel with any grace from a large-diameter skein. A 3-yard (2.7 m) cotton single skein at 10,000 yards/pound (9,144 meters/.45 kilogram) will be a challenge to unwind. The skein is too large for most lightweight swifts. Larger-circumference swifts weigh too much to unreel the fine cotton without breaking it. The trick is to use lightweight winding gear that runs easily for a skein of that size.[23] The rest of us mere mortals wind smaller-diameter and less-bulky fine yarn skeins.

Heavier plied yarns can be wound in 3-yard (2.7 m) skeins or larger. Linen and hemp singles yarns are often strong enough to unwind from these large diameter skeins. If your winding gear makes this size skein, then try lightweight skeins, which you can gradually increase in bulk as you become comfortable with what your gear can handle.

If you count the turns on your niddy-noddy or reel, you have half the information to figure the size or "grist" of your yarn. To get the last half, put your dry, boiled skein on a scale. Doing so gives you the relationship of length of skein to its weight, which is its grist—for example 50 yards/ounce (45.7 m/28.3 g).

---

23 A solution to this problem is to have the swift powered, not free running, and to match the rate of delivery to the winding rate.

How Winding Off Affects Twist

The form (skein, bobbin, cone, ball) of your yarn can affect the twist in your yarn when you unwind it. This is a function of whether the form is side delivery or end feed. Side delivery means that the yarn comes at right angles to a turning axis. The yarn form has to turn to unwind the yarn. End-feed forms do not need to turn. The yarn peels over the end of the form. Bobbins, spools, and skeins can be side delivery forms. Center-pull balls and cones are end feed.

If you want to see what happens with these two delivery systems, take a spool of ribbon and lay it flat on the table. Pull the ribbon off the spool by pulling it up, over the edge of the spool. The ribbon moves around the perimeter of the spool. Note that for each circuit, the ribbon is twisted once.

Now, pick up the spool, hold it in one hand and pull the ribbon straight off the spool, not over the edges. The spool rotates as the ribbon comes off without a twist.

What this means is that end-feed yarn packages add twist in the yarn, one turn for each track around the package. Let's take a closer look. Let's assume you have a center-pull ball that's 3" (7.5 cm) across. If you unwind it from the outside, for each trip around the ball (3" [7.5 cm] times pi, or 3.14), or every 9" (23 cm) or so, the yarn gets one additional twist. If you take the yarn from the inside, you'll get different numbers. If the core is 1" (2.5 cm) in diameter, each trip puts in one turn but now it's every 3" (7.5 cm) instead of every 9" (23 cm). That's three times as much added twist when the yarn is pulled from the center rather than from the outside of this ball.

Bobbins, spools, and skeins feed from the sides.

Center-pull balls and cones feed from the ends.

Ribbon will form a twist for each rotation when unwound from the top, as will end-feed preparations.

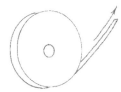

Ribbon will not twist if it's pulled straight off the spool, as for side-delivery preparations.

Note that the change will either add or subtract twist. Imagine that the center-pull ball is a miniature earth. If you see the hole in the ball as the north/south axis of the globe and pull yarn from the north end, you may add twist. If that's the case, you can be sure that if you pull it out the south end, you'll remove twist. There's no rule that the north end of the ball adds twist; the rule is simply that one end adds twist and the other removes it. This applies to all center-pull balls.

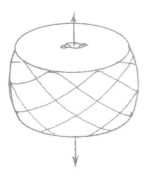

Pulling yarn from one end of a center-pull ball will add twist, while pulling from the other end will subtract twist. But there's no predicting which direction will add twist and which will will remove it.

Can this change really have much effect? The answer is yes, in some instances. Very stiff yarns, such as hemp, linen, mohair, the camelids, and high-twist yarns, can be intolerant of changes in twist.[24] Large, softly spun yarns sustain change in twist with better grace. In these twist-sensitive yarns, removing twist from the ply structure can result in a seriously lively yarn.

Setting the Twist

COTTON, FLAX, AND HEMP need to be boiled in a soapy solution to set the twist.

Here's the recipe:

Fill a large nonreactive pot (steel, glass, or enamel, not iron) three-quarters full with tap water. Add 1 tablespoon of a simple dry laundry detergent that contains no enzymes, fluorescent dyes, or bleach. Then add 2 tablespoons washing soda (soda ash) and mix thoroughly.

Put your yarn in the pot and place the pot on a heat source. Simmer for 30 to 45 minutes, taking care not to let the pot boil dry (if this happens, the yarn will be worthless).

After simmering, pull the yarn from the pot and rinse it under a stream of running water. Cool water isn't a problem. The cellulosics won't felt.

You want to make sure that the yarn dries quickly. If the yarns remain in a damp condition, mildew will attack the yarn and significantly reduce its strength. Gently squeeze excess water out of the cones of cotton and skeins of linen and hemp yarn. You can also put the yarn into lingerie or laundry bags and then into the spin cycle of your washing machine. Or you can wuzz them the old-fashioned way.[25] Flip a towel through the skeins to straighten the yarn and remove remaining moisture. Hang the skeins out in the breeze and sunlight to finish drying.

Did you notice the color of the wash water when you pulled your yarn? This alone should encourage you to wash your yarn before using it. When the yarn is dry, see how limp and lovely the cotton yarns have become. The hemp and linen yarns will continue to soften and will become whiter with each wash.

---

24 These same yarns can be close to impossible to weave with an end-feed shuttle.

25 Wuzzing involves slinging the water out of the yarn by twirling it in a bag—a sort of strong-arm hydro-extraction.

Preparing to Dye

WHILE YOUR YARN IS IN SKEIN FORM, maybe still wet from scouring, you have the option to dye it before plying (if you plan to), knitting, or weaving. Of course, you can dye the plied yarn, or dye the finished fabric, or dye even later for different results. However, this point in the process is a good time to discuss getting your yarn ready to dye, and the dyes to use on cotton, linen, and hemp yarns.

Your yarn should be in loosely tied skeins. If the ties are too tight, the dye can't penetrate the yarn, and will leave a light spot.

Any fiber must be clean for it to take dye well. Cotton is mostly free of its natural oils and waxes after the first good boiling scour. Flax and hemp have more durable oils and waxes than cotton. Any left on the yarn can keep the dye from adhering to the fiber, making the yarn appear dirty or spotty. If you dye flax or hemp before it's scoured clean, the dye floats off in the wash along with other soluble greases and pectin. The dye rubs off on your hands, your tools, and whatever else it comes in contact with. This is a nasty situation known as "crocking." Unfortunately, this situation can't be "saved" by soaking your skeins in salt or vinegar (even worse for the fibers damaged by acids!). It results from the fiber not being clean at the start.

Besides waxes and oils, hemp has the added challenge of lignin. The red lignin gives hemp fiber a manila color. Sometimes it takes multiple boiling scours to whiten linen and hemp.[26]

Types of Dyes

The subject of dyeing cotton, flax, and hemp is extensive enough for a book of its own. Here we can only tease with hors d'oeuvres. Three cellulose dye families are of interest to the home dyer: vat, fiber reactive, and natural source dyes.

Historically, **vat dyes** were used extensively on cotton, linen, and hemp. Vat-dyed yarns are both washfast and lightfast. The most familiar of the vat dyes is indigo. Maintenance of an indigo vat was once a trade secret, as much an art as science. Now, vat dyes and the information needed to use them are as close as your Internet connection. And these dyes are easy to use in many colors besides indigo.[27]

Fiber-reactive dyes are also reasonably lightfast and washfast, with an inspired palette of colors. Because they're cold-water dyes, you don't need any special range-top setup. I've dyed pounds of fiber and yarn outside in plastic tubs, even in winter. (Yes, you can dye in the refrigerator.) It goes more slowly, but there's no gas bill. For many years, fiber-reactive dyes were sold under the Procion label, but now many

Tie the skein loosely so the dye can penetrate the yarn under the ties.

---

26 Lignin is in both flax and hemp, but in hemp it's tenacious. It can take up to a dozen boiling scours to make hemp white. When it isn't white, the tinged base color affects any applied color. Pale lilac turns muddy gray. A cool mint green results, instead, in light olive green.

27 Inko screen vat dyes were used on Grateful Dead t-shirts because of their brilliant strong colors.

companies produce these easy-to-use dyes. As with the vat dyes, information about current sources and instructions are online.

Natural-source dyes fall into two categories: those that dye cellulosic yarns directly, known as "substantive" (the substance is the dye), and those that need an assist or "additive."

It's possible to dye with natural plant materials such as walnut hulls, oak galls, almond hulls, cotton leaves, tea, coffee, and sumac. These substantive dyes are often rich in tannin, which, on its own, acts as a mordant (see below). It's a simple process: simmer the dye material in water until the water is strongly colored, strain the dye liquor, then immerse wetted skeins in it. After a gentle simmer and rinse, cellulose yarns turn soft pastels: beige, gold, peach, yellow, light charcoal, or sepia.

Natural-source dyes need a mordant to give a stronger and more enduring hue. Mordants are used with additive natural dyestuffs such as madder, cochineal, weld, logwood, cutch, and Brazilwood. Mordants are metallic salts[28] that bond the dye to the fiber. The mordants are applied to the yarn, sometimes in conjunction with dyeing them, sometimes before, and sometimes after. Each process produces different effects. On protein fibers, a single mordant bath may be all that's necessary to fix the dye onto the fiber. Cotton, linen, and hemp require three separate mordant baths: first alum, then tannin, then alum again. This time-consuming process produces colors as rich and complex as the flavors of a proper red wine.

---

28 Five of the most common mordants are potassium aluminum sulfate (alum), ferrous sulfate (iron), stannous chloride (tin), potassium dichromate (chrome), and copper sulfate (copper).

Bleaching Linen and Hemp

Why isn't there some magic potion that will bleach linen and hemp white so you can stop all this fooling around with boiling pots of water and get on with dyeing? There are, of course, chemical bleaches, but they take a terrible toll on the strength and durability of bast fibers. I've seen chemically bleached sheets and pillowcases so tender you could put your finger through them. Linens should last for hundreds of years and will, if treated well. Consider that you may have spun line flax finely and intend to weave or knit something destined to become an heirloom. Is it worth it to rush for a solution to bleach this yarn?

The alternative to chemical bleaching is to boil your yarns, then put them out in the sunlight to dry. They will not suffer from this treatment—in fact, they'll become softer and whiter with each boil and dance in the sun.

Plying

THERE ARE DISTINCT BENEFITS to be gained from plying yarns.

First and foremost, you'll end up with larger (thicker) yarns. Yes, you could have spun larger singles. But spinning large singles from the cellulose fibers is not an easy task, and maintaining a consistent yarn at that size is an art. Not only is it easier to produce a larger yarn with plied singles, but the plied yarn wears better. It is more abrasion-resistant because each single has greater twist than a single of the same size as the plied yarn. The added twist makes the plied yarn stronger and less prone to snagging.

Second, plying will give a cellulose yarn something that it doesn't naturally possess: elasticity.

And finally, you can use the structure of plied yarns for color effects. In its simplest application, you can form a barber-pole yarn—one ply each of two colors in a two-ply yarn. The possibilities expand with each additional ply. Try combining one colored ply with three natural plies to make an attractive fleck or spot pattern in a four-strand cable yarn (two 2-ply yarns). The finer the singles, the greater the number of plies that can be combined, and the more possibilities you'll have for powerful color effects in "optical blending."

Plying Setup

Place the bobbins from which you wish to ply as far away from the spinning wheel orifice as you can manage. Doing so will even out the twist in the singles *and* give you a chance to deal with any untoward yarn behavior while plying.

You'll want to keep your bobbins from playing out too much yarn. When indiscriminate amounts of yarn are released, the longer yarn will kink back on itself and will lead to much

fiddling and start-and-stop plying, which isn't a happy technique. It's better to have some way to keep the bobbins from freely casting out excess yarn. One solution is a lazy kate in which the bobbins are slowed with some type of brake mechanism. Most often, this technique is similar to the scotch tension brake—a string attached to an adjustable spring.

Another kate style puts the bobbins on vertical spikes. The weight of the bobbin slows them down and keeps them from overrunning extra yarn. And a third setup uses a "gate" to slow the yarn. Place a smooth coffee mug between you and the lazy kate, then thread one yarn around one side of the mug and through the handle (which points at your spinning wheel). Thread the other yarn around the other side of the mug and around the other side of the handle. Doing so causes the mug to act like a gate, forcing the yarns to curve around the body of the cup and past the handle. The added minor friction does the job.

PLYING SETUP

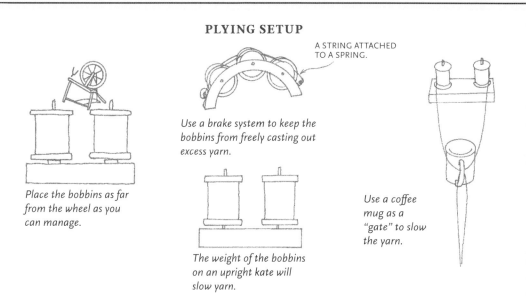

A STRING ATTACHED TO A SPRING.

Place the bobbins as far from the wheel as you can manage.

Use a brake system to keep the bobbins from freely casting out excess yarn.

The weight of the bobbins on an upright kate will slow yarn.

Use a coffee mug as a "gate" to slow the yarn.

PLYING ON A WHEEL

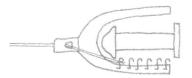

Tie the ends of the two yarns together, thread them through the orifice, and slip the knot onto the first hook.

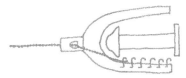

Treadle to create about 12" (30.5 cm) of plied yarn.

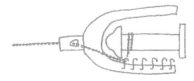

Tie the yarn to the bobbin core.

Use your flyer hand to pinch off the twist while your bobbin hand stretches back toward the bobbins.

Close your bobbin hand down on the two yarns, slowly open your flyer hand, and let the twist travel between your hands.

Step-by-Step Plying

For conventional yarns, ply two yarns of similar twist in the opposite direction from which they were spun. Spin Z and ply S. Or spin S and ply Z.

To begin, pull the ends of two yarns off the bobbins, pair them together, and tie a knot near their ends. Thread the two yarns through the orifice of the flyer and slip the knotted end over the first flyer hook.

Treadle until the yarn looks like it's beaded (for cotton) or firmly twisted (for flax and hemp) for about 12" (30.5 cm) of plied yarn.

Unhook the knot from the flyer, pass the yarn around a hook, and tie it to the bobbin core.

Turn the bobbin to wrap the yarn on itself a couple of times. You're ready to ply.

Use your flyer hand to pinch off the twist while your bobbin hand stretches back along the yarns toward the bobbins.

Close your bobbin hand down on the two yarns, then slowly open your flyer hand and let twist travel between your hands.

Bring your flyer hand toward your bobbin hand, along the ply twist, while your bobbin hand remains closed on the yarns and moves toward your flyer hand (allowing some wind-on of plied yarn).

As the two hands almost touch, close your flyer hand on the plied yarn and move slowly toward the flyer (winding on the plied yarn). Slide your bobbin hand along the yarn and back toward the bobbins (this is easier to do than to describe).

Repeat this process, closing your bobbin hand on the two yarns while slowly opening your flyer hand and letting the twist travel between your hands. Begin to move your bobbin hand toward your flyer hand, and so it goes.

If you watched this activity from somewhere near the ceiling, the spinner would seem to spread both arms apart, then bring them together in front of him/herself. The flyer hand first pinches off the twist as the bobbin hand straightens out the two unplied yarns. The bobbin hand then pinches off the twist and the flyer hand opens and lets twist between the hands. The bobbin hand moves toward the flyer hand, and plied yarn winds onto the wheel.

When all is going well, the bobbins on the lazy kate never stop turning, the wheel is constantly winding on a bit of plied yarn, and all is right with the world.

Bring your hands together.

Move your flyer hand toward the flyer to wind on the plied yarn while you slide your bobbin hand back toward the bobbins.

Setting the Plied Yarn

It's likely that your plied yarn will be lively (also called "active") after plying and will need to be set. Wash it according to the detergent/washing soda recipe on page 127. Linen and hemp yarns can be boiled in the skein. Cotton yarns are often much easier to handle when they're plied and can be set in the skein. It's also possible to wind them onto cones and boil them on the cone. Just accept that all this boiling before you use your yarn will make the bast fibers that much softer, whiter, and easier to knit and dispense from a shuttle bobbin. Your cottons will likewise be more compliant.

***Boiled hemp yarn** (left) is softer and whiter than* ***unboiled hemp yarn** (right).*

Some Plied Yarn Ideas

To make a more elastic cotton yarn, you'll want to spin high-twist singles. Then ply them in the same direction as they were spun. Take two of these yarns and ply them in the conventional ply direction in a method called "cabling." In other words, make a cabled yarn by spinning singles in the Z direction, plying them in the Z direction, then cable-plying them in the S direction. Boil the cabled yarn in the skein under no tension. The yarn will bulk up and be somewhat more elastic.

The End of the Yarn

'I CAN HEAR IT NOW. You were saying to yourself, "But what I want to do is spin! I just got it going. I don't want to stop!" Boy, can I understand wanting to stay "in the groove."

Just as there is sublime meditation in comfortable spinning, there is a quiet, compelling quality in the act of winding off your yarn. You'll relive moments taken to make the yarn while automatically checking for weak spots in the yarn and daydreaming about its future. In time, you'll anticipate the change that comes over your yarn when you set the twist. You'll see your fresh yarn as the pupa still in the cocoon, ready to open up and spread its wings, and become. With unequalled pride and sense of accomplishment gathering around your shoulders, you'll watch the pile of skeins grow.

Shall we put these yarns to use? Yes, let's.

CHAPTER FIVE:

Knitting with the Enemy

5

Spinners more familiar with wool are often put off by their first attempts to knit with linen, hemp, and cotton yarns. However, knitting with plant–fiber yarns has advantages. The yarns' sterling attributes include the fact that they won't shrink or felt when you wash them, won't pill, and won't attract moths and carpet beetles. In addition, these yarns take a lot of hard wear and show little change, much less damage. So why do knitters give linen and hemp the "fish eye"? It may be that they're unfamiliar with the plant fibers.

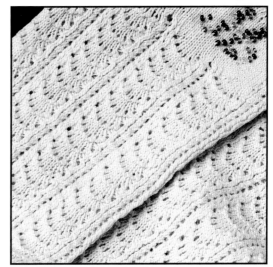

These cotton stockings date back to the Civil War.

Cotton, linen, and hemp share a hallmark characteristic that's foreign to most knitters: inelasticity. This quality utterly transforms the way these yarns are perceived and used, as well as the character of the resulting fabrics. Knitters who use only woolen-type yarns sometimes avoid the plant-fiber challenges. Intruth, the bast fibers spin and knit much like worsted-spun hair fibers, such as adult mohair, yak, and camel hair. But not too many knitters use those fibers. Cotton and the fine hairs—cashmere, angora rabbit, alpaca, and qiviut—have similarities. Have you ever been surprised by how an angora or alpaca yarn knits up? They aren't the same as wool, are they?

Besides having little stretch, plant yarns are lean, with no loft or bulk. The stitches don't swell with fluff and fill in the empty spaces. Instead of being soft, freshly handspun linen

Note the nice stitch definition in this detail of a lace shawl knitted from nettle yarn.

and hemp yarns knit as if they were stiff wire. They slither off the needles when you do no more than pick up your work. Then, when you finally get them knitted up, the fabric is boardlike. And the fabric isn't even warm! The knitting needles fly back into the basket and the exasperated spinner is left wondering "Why am I knitting with the enemy?"

Perceived Drawbacks and How to Overcome Them

A DISCUSSION OF DESIGNING with plant fiber–based yarns is definitely in order (take a big deep breath). A successful designer looks to the essential character of raw materials, then accepts their benefits and works with their liabilities. However, the negative aspects often can be reduced, modified, or seen in a new context that makes them assets. Nestled among the difficult aspects of designing with plant fiber–based yarns are opportunities to expand your experience, shift your expectations, and review your primary assumptions. You just might change your mind.

Let's take another look at these complaints from a designer's point of view, and deal with them one by one.

Lack of Elasticity

As wool knitters, we're used to knitting with elastic yarns. That doesn't mean that we should only knit springy stuff. Firm yarn can be just the thing for a sturdy market bag, an entryway mat, a trivet for the table, or a scrubby cloth for the bath. At times, firm, inelastic yarns are the better choice.

Once you've decided to venture into this perhaps uncharted realm, you can choose to do a few things that that will make your job easier.

Adjust Your Needles and Gauge

It's beneficial to open up your gauge when you knit with inelastic yarns such as cotton, linen, and hemp. A loose, open gauge lets you maneuver the yarn around the needles and do complex stitches with plenty of room in each stitch to accommodate the two needle tips. One way to open your gauge is to pick larger needles than you would use with wools. Certainly you'll need to swatch and sample to get what you want.

If you cast on cellulosic yarns firmly enough to grip your needles, you'll find them too tight to knit. So cast on loosely or on larger needles, then switch to smaller needles for the body of the project. The cast-on stitches will tend to bag on the needles and slip off easily. Use tip protectors to prevent that from happening.

Choose your knitting needles based on their degree of slickness. Needles with a more "grabby" surface, such as plastic or bamboo needles, will tend to stay in place better than highly polished steel ones. Until you develop your gauge when knitting with these yarns, save your wooden, casein, or bone needles. Yes, they have good surfaces, but while you're discovering your gauge with these yarns, you may apply considerable pressure to the needles' tips; I wouldn't want you to damage your fine ones. Instead, the most commonplace needles seem to handle plant-source yarns with grace, courage, and vigor.

Also consider the shape of the needle tips. Rounded tips don't work as well for me as those with long hollow-ground or concave tapered tips. Concave tips might work better for you, too. I encourage you to start out with a small project, such as a washcloth. Doing

Flax fibers make firm yarns that knit into sturdy market bags.

Because they stand up well to heat, moisture, and detergents, plant fibers make ideal washcloths.

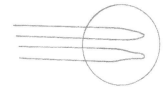
***Rounded needle tips** (top) don't work as well for me as those with long hollow-ground or **concave tapered tips** (bottom).*

so will give you a chance to modify and settle into your "new gauge" before you embark on a large project.

Choose an Elastic Stitch Pattern

You can choose stitch patterns that instill elasticity. For example, knit-one-purl-one (k1, p1) ribbing is much more elastic than stockinette stitch, no matter the fiber content of the yarn. However, once stretched, the cellulose yarn will not recover its original size or shape. Instead, these yarns tend to sag. Although this quality may not be as desirable in a garment, it can be a positive attribute in a market bag or hammock.

To prevent ribbing from gaping at the cuff, hem, or neckline of a garment, try knitting a strand of elastic along with the cellulosic yarn. Or try substituting seed stitch, mock twisted cables, or an I-cord (also called knit-cord) edge. Or eliminate the need for ribbing by choosing a design that doesn't rely on elastic cuffs, neckline, or hems. Instead, consider a rolled edge of pure stockinette stitch. These choices aren't about limitations, but possibilities!

Change the Garment Design

Because cotton, flax, and hemp have so little elasticity, you could start out with a garment pattern that has a looser, "sweatshirt" or kimono type of fit, with lower armscyes and relaxed necklines, sleeves, and hems. As you become more familiar with the ease or lack thereof in these yarns, consider designing pattern pieces as if they were flat patterns for woven garments. There will be some elasticity in a piece that measures 26" (66 cm) wide, but nowhere near as much as that for worsted-weight wool.

Before you begin to knit a project, such as a hat, knit a swatch in the stitch pattern you intend to use, measure the gauge on the swatch, and

The garter ridges "pop" in this short-row linen bag.

I added elastic thread to keep the ribbing snug in these linen socks.

measure the head you want to fit. Figure casting on the same number of stitches as the length you need minus about 1 to 2 percent, allowing for full stitch-pattern multiples. My point is that because these yarns have virtually no elasticity, you'll want to cast on fewer stitches than you would when knitting with an elastic wool yarn of the same size. You want the cotton, linen, or flax yarn to have to stretch to fit.

Cellulosic Yarns Don't Full

Unlike their woolly counterparts, cotton, linen, and hemp yarns are flat. They don't bloom, felt, or compact. Lean and lustrous, linen and hemp yarns highlight fabric architecture. They make stitch patterns "pop"; each stitch stands out in a clear statement of structure. Even the misshapen stitches.

Bast fibers don't hide the knitted structure—instead, they track it openly, with breathtaking directness. For this reason, bast-fiber yarns demand a scrupulous knitting technique. There's no place to hide mistakes. In return, your work—your struggle to spin, design, and knit with this yarn—will become an eloquent travelogue of your "road less taken."

After washing and boiling, manipulating and laundering, bast yarns become soft and very wearable.

Because bast yarns are so different from typical woolen knitting yarns, you have the opportunity to revisit knitting patterns. Two-color, knit-purl, short-row, slipped-stitch patterns, and so many more, offer new dimensions, directions, and possibilities when worked with cotton, linen, or hemp yarns.

Cellulosic Yarns Are Stiff

We don't often think of the effects of time on knitted fabrics, but bast fibers are long-lived and change with each dunk in the suds. Freshly spun, they are wiry and stiff, but when washed and boiled, linen and hemp become much softer. After they're manipulated and beetled, they soften even more. With each laundering, they'll lose stiffness and become whiter. They'll never turn as soft as cotton, but they do soften and lose their wiry character.[29]

---

29 After washing, cotton has its own moment of stiffness until it's manipulated. When tossed into the tumble dryer, we don't see this stiffness. However, think about line-dried towels. Snap them when they are damp-dry, and they suddenly become much softer.

How to Soften Bast Fibers

Because these fibers soften with use, they will soften even as you knit them. You can hasten the change before you pick up your needles through a sequence of boiling, freezing, defrosting, pounding, and then doing it all again. But if you plan to ply your yarn, be sure to do so before you begin this softening process.

First, wind the yarn into a skein, tie the end to the beginning, and tie any loose ties several places around the skein to prevent the yarn from tangling.

Give the skein a boiling scour as if to wash it (use 1 tablespoon washing soda and 2 tablespoons laundry detergent in a big soup pot of water).

Simmer on low heat for 20 to 30 minutes.

Rinse in warmish water until the water runs clear and the skein is no longer slippery.

Squeeze excess water from skein, pop it in a plastic bag, and put it in the freezer.

After the yarn is fully frozen, remove it from freezer to thaw.

Hang the skein to dry.

Pound the skein with a smooth-faced mallet against a clean board. The mallet should have rounded edges, not sharp ones like typical iron hammers. Use a wooden flax-beetling mallet or a "dead-blow" plastic-covered mallet. The luster will improve as you pound the yarn.

Repeat the boiling, rinsing, freezing, and pounding sequence until the dried yarn is suitably soft.

It may take six or seven sequences to make the skein hang limp in your hand. Knitting with this yarn will be easier, friendlier, and similar to knitting with cotton. However, keep in mind that even this rigorous process won't

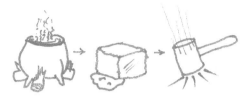

Boil, freeze, and pound bast fibers to soften them.

This woven cotton scarf drapes beautifully.

make the yarn elastic. It just isn't possible with cellulosic fibers.

As cellulosic yarns undergo subsequent launderings, they become less stiff. Cotton relaxes and becomes softer. Thus, the drape of these yarns improves with each washing. Will they develop the drape of silk or wool? No. They will have the distinctive drape of cotton, linen, and hemp.

This sheer cotton keffiyeh stays wrapped around my neck because the cotton sticks to itself.

"feel" each linen or hemp yarn as distinct and separate. This backbone is an essential part of the crisp body of a linen fabric.

The Importance of Size

THE SIZE OF YOUR YARN will affect how well it performs. Large (thick) cellulosic yarns don't behave well because they're stiffer and more easily soiled than finer ones. This may seem counter-intuitive but, in a garment, they will fail sooner than finer yarns and fabrics. The missing piece to this puzzle is "twist." Finer yarns have more twist. You can knit them with more stitches and more contact points per inch (2.5 cm). These yarns and structures are less likely to abrade, snag, and attract soil.

Cotton tends to cling to other fibers, and even more tenaciously to other cotton fibers. Sheer cottons may float with a loft similar to silk, but give them an adjacent cotton fabric, and they'll grab on. This is a good thing if you want your scarf to stay wrapped on your head. If you want the buoyant fling of Ginger Rogers' skirts, you're barking up the wrong plant fiber. Sorry, silk is *the* solution for that one.

In time, linen and hemp will develop a drape much like chamois or suede. They lose their wiriness but never seem to lose their definition. Bast yarns always have a "backbone." One old-fashioned test for the difference between a cotton and linen handkerchief is to run your fingernail across the face of the fabric with your thumb beneath the cloth. Cotton yarns feel soft and they mush into the overall body of the cloth. Your fingernail will

These hemp bags might just last forever.

In finer yarns, the essential qualities—absorbency, smoothness, softness, and strength—are also increased. If you choose to knit with cellulosic fibers, then know that when you spin them into thick yarns, you'll sacrifice these qualities. An 800 yard-per-pound (7,315 m/.45 kg) linen yarn will never drape like one at 3,200 yards per pound (2,926 m/.45 kg). It doesn't matter how many times you wash the larger yarn. It's the stuff of burlap and burlap it will remain. If you need a thicker knitting yarn, ply several fine strands together. Your plied yarn will retain all the good qualities of a fine yarn, only it will be thicker.

Most of the reasons to ply wool yarns don't apply to cotton, linen, or hemp. Wool yarns are plied to improve elasticity, strength, and warmth. Cotton isn't elastic, but it's already strong, is going to be cool, and if you attempt to make it fuzzy and lofty, you'll have trouble keeping the fibers from shedding and clogging the lint trap in your washing machine.

"But, but, but," you say, "I don't like knitting on tiny needles." If this is the case, ply your yarn so you can knit on the needle size you prefer. Just realize that as any cellulosic yarn grows in size, its behavior approaches that of string. Linen yarn suitable to be knitted on U.S. size 2 or 3 (2.75 or 3.25 mm) needles is a different critter from a yarn suitable for U.S. size 8 or 10 (5 or 6 mm) needles.

Finishing Cotton, Flax, and Hemp Knits

ᴀFTER YOU BIND OFF THE last row of cotton, linen, or hemp yarns, you'll want to work in the loose ends of yarn before you assemble the pieces. Then, you'll need to relax the stresses imparted by the knitting. It will be much easier to assemble and finish your piece if you relax those stresses by putting the knitted pieces into an additional boiling scour.

These two washcloths were knitted from the same bast yarn. The whiter, softer washcloth on the right has been boiled.

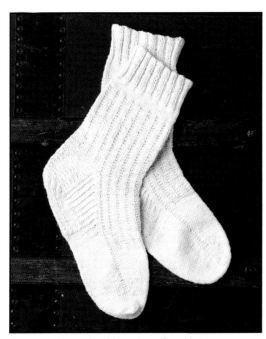

Cotton socks are durable and comfortable in warm weather.

You'll follow the same procedure you used before:

- ❀ Put 1 tablespoon of washing soda, 2 tablespoons of laundry detergent, and the knitted pieces in a large pot.

- ❀ Bring the pot to a boil and simmer for 20 minutes.

- ❀ Rinse in warm running water.

- ❀ Pin the pieces flat on a towel to dry.

- ❀ Steam-press the dry pieces on the steam setting for cotton.

If you iron the pieces as well, using steam for cotton or a hot setting for dampened linen or hemp, then tricky or elaborate constructions will go much easier.

The vast repertoire of knitwear includes garments meant to keep us warm throughout the fall, winter, and spring. Knitting with cellulosic fibers, however, gives you the chance to design summertime coolers for feet, head, and body. Cool linen socks, lacy summer nighties, broad-brimmed hats, and smooth pillow shams and cases are just a few of the possibilities that come to mind. Not only can these plant fiber pieces be graceful as garments or accessories, but in steamy summertime weather, they can become your personal air conditioner.

After scores of washings, this combined filet-mesh and woven nightgown only gets softer and more comfortable.

CHAPTER SIX:

Weaving Yarns & Tales

6

The previous chapters have concentrated on spinning unfamiliar materials, the goal being to have you become knowledgeable and comfortable as you transform them into yarn. The "construction" portion of the lesson is behind us. This final chapter looks at yarn design from a weaver's point of view. It concludes with suggestions about the tools, choices, and modifications that can make the weaving process easier.

When it's time to put yarn on the loom, we begin to see it in a different light. Questions arise. Will I be able to use the same yarns for weaving as for knitting? What makes a good warp yarn? What about the weft yarn? Will the process of weaving affect the yarn's appearance? Its functionality? What qualities will shine through in the cloth? These questions encompass a vital component of good design—how our yarns perform.

Yarn for weaving is quite different than that for knitting. Many knitters favor a yarn that is springy, soft, and open. Bend a typical knitting yarn over your finger and watch it stretch and get thinner. Full of air pockets and elasticity, this yarn will knit up into something warm and comfortable. However, if the same yarn were woven instead, the qualities that make it a delightful knitting yarn will make it challenging to work with. You may also find yourself disappointed with the spongy hand of the woven fabric.

Warp Yarn Characteristics

FROM AN ARCHITECTURAL point of view, warp yarn must withstand the rigors of weaving with little damage or change. Four qualities make a good warp yarn—inelasticity, integrity, size, and abrasion resistance.

Inelasticity

A yarn that's appropriate for a warp yarn will hardly stretch when pulled and bent over your finger, and it will show little change in size. This is a good thing. Warp yarn goes on the loom under tension and is woven under tension. For the cloth to have consistent density, the tension should be the same across the width and length of the cloth. Inelastic yarn is easier to put on the loom with reasonable consistency, and easier to weave off.

Integrity

Warp yarns, singles or plied, should be spun firmly so they won't drift apart under tension. They must endure changing tensions as the shed opens and closes, which exerts a "tug and release" on each strand of yarn every time a new shed is opened or a treadle is tromped. If the yarn has no integrity, it will lengthen a bit with each tug. A warp yarn not held under the same tension as its neighbors will droop into the open shed and become abraded, snagged, and ultimately torn by the passing shuttle. The only way to manage this situation is to replace the drifty warp end.

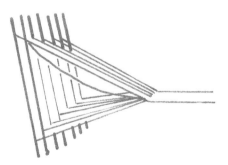

A warp yarn not held under the same tension as its neighbors will droop into the open shed and become abraded.

Size

A warp yarn needs to be of a size that will fit through the reed and heddle eyes. Reeds come in different spacings from four to fifty (or more) dents per inch (2.5 cm). This range makes it possible to weave from thick to fine yarns. With an assortment of reeds, you can weave a wide range of yarn sizes. Heddles are available in standard and large-eyed types, so if you want to weave with thick yarn, you'll want to use ones with large eyes. It's important to note that if you want a flat cloth, then you'll want to use yarns with the same grist and twist. Thick yarns combined with thin, or soft-spun yarns combined with firm crêpe yarns will produce a highly textured cloth.

Abrasion Resistance

The structure and surface of a warp yarn needs to resist abrasion in the reed. Any hairiness will tend to increase with each pass of the reed and eventually raise a nap on the yarn. As the nap grows longer, fibers can come off the yarn and form "doughnuts" around the reed blade. This obstructs the yarn's passage through the reed and hastens its failure.

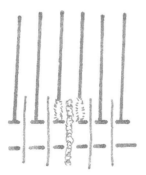

Hairy warp yarns will form "doughnuts" around the reed blades.

The natural characteristics of flax, hemp, and cotton make them perfect for weaving. The yarns are inelastic. The fibers are readily spun into fine yarns that are, by nature, extremely strong. Fine cotton is adequately abrasion resistant, and linen and hemp are supremely so. Voilà!

Weft Yarn Characteristics

'WEFT YARNS DON'T NEED to be stretched on a loom, rubbed by a reed or beater, or pulled up and down while weaving. The demands placed on them are simple. To wit: weft yarns need to feed easily off the shuttle, be it a stick, ski, boat, or end-feed style. Although it's possible to pass weft yarn without using a shuttle, it's precious slow work. If your yarn won't behave coming off the shuttle, then set the twist, size the yarn, take greater care winding the shuttle, choose another shuttle, or choose a different weft yarn. Do something, because weaving without a shuttle is on par with sweeping the floor with a clothes brush. It can be done, but why?

More on Yarn Structure

'WEAVING YARNS DO NOT NEED to be plied. Linen and hemp are naturally strong. Plying to "improve their strength" isn't necessary. Consistent fine cotton yarns are likewise strong. The reasons for plying cellulosics are to achieve a particular size, to blend colors, or to achieve the texture of a plied yarn.

Abrasion of warp yarns is often more pronounced at the selvedges, but it can occur anywhere across the width of the cloth. Knots and novelty yarns are particularly vulnerable

145

to this abrasion, shifting and sliding along with the reed or untying completely. Knots are best untied and replaced as you would a broken warp end. You should avoid unstable bouclé and knop yarns in the warp.

Omitted from our discussion are several major design aspects: color, texture, and yarn size (except in the broadest sense). These decisions are more than aesthetic choices; they also affect how satisfied you are with the finished piece, how often you'll use it, and how long it lasts. These are, however, beyond the scope of this practical guide.

Dressing the Loom

SOME CHOICES MAKE FOR A SWEETER weaving experience. For example, a sound, well-spun singles is a good choice for both warp and weft. Linen or hemp singles can be strong, abrasion-resistant, and inelastic. The same is true of cotton singles. The secret to using singles as warp is in the sizing.

Sizing the Warp

Sizing is a glue or paste (see box at right for recipes) applied to the yarn to smooth the surface, reduce the diameter of the yarn, and keep it from losing twist if broken during weaving. Sizing is best applied to the yarn while in skein form. Simply dunk your skein into the sizing mixture, wring out the excess liquid, then wind the skein onto a blocking reel to dry. When it's dry, wind the skein onto a spool and wind your warp from that. The sized warp will be so stiff that you won't need a sley or reed hook to pass the cut ends through the reed and heddles.

A good sizing mixture readily washes out in soap and water. It's there when you need it, and graciously departs when you don't.

Sizing Recipes

Here are three recipes for sizing solutions. Each recipe makes 1 pint.

BOILED FLOUR

This is a thick, multipurpose sizing that works as well on wool as well as cotton. It's somewhat slow drying with little tendency to drip.

- ½ cup all-purpose flour
- 2 cups water

Make a paste of the flour with a small portion of the water. When smooth, add 1 cup of water and bring to a boil slowly, stirring constantly. Reduce heat and stir until the mixture becomes pearly translucent. Take care—this mixture can scorch easily. Add remaining water and stir until smooth.

GELATIN

This is a runny solution, so watch for pooling on your yarn. It dries quickly.

- 2 tablespoons (2 packets) unflavored gelatin
- ¼ cup cold water
- 1 cup boiling water
- ¾ cup cold water

Soak gelatin in cold water until it swells. Stir in boiling water until gelatin dissolves. Add cold water and stir.

MILK

This solution is also runny, so beware of pooling and dripping. (It's much favored by family felines.)

- 1 packet (for 1 quart) instant nonfat milk
- 2 cups cool water

Stir powdered milk into water until mixed.

Setts for Handspun Yarns

Like the subtleties of knitting gauge, sett—how close together the warp ends are placed—will have a significant effect on the finished cloth. It's always a good idea to weave a sample before embarking on a full-size project. Fortunately, there is a mathematical model—Ashenhurst's Formula (see page 156—that provides ballpark guidelines for where to begin. I always whip out my pocket calculator and use this formula when I set out to sample. But to save you time and energy, I've included a table of suggested yarn grists and setts for plain weave and 2/2 twill on page 156. The suggested setts factor in yarn softness and loom variations, but assume that you'll use the same yarn for warp and weft in a balanced weave in which there are the same number of picks per inch as there are ends per inch.

To save time, measure and label each skein as you wind it off your wheel or spindle. Include the number of yards and weight of the skein. Doing so provides a record of this vital information, even if you only note yards per gram or wraps on the niddy per 100th of an ounce. You can always sit down later with a pocket calculator and a cup of tea to figure the number of yards per pound (meters per kilogram).

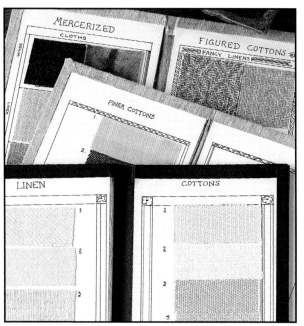

My replica eighteenth-century sample books.

Label your skeins for reference.

Reeds, Heddles & Looms

Reeds can be sleyed with one end or multiple ends per slot. Handspun cotton, hemp, and linen work well if sleyed with multiple ends in each dent. In other words, sley two ends of linen in each dent of an 8-dent reed instead of sleying singly in a 16-dent reed. Grouping more ends in each dent will reduce the amount of abrasion. You could say it spreads the load.

As for **heddles**, twisted wire heddles can be the most challenging. The bottom and top of each wire eye is twisted in such a way that it can catch a hairy or irregular yarn. Flat steel heddles, which have relatively smooth eyes and can nest together for fine setts, are good choices. The inserted-eye heddle, which is both lightweight (like a wire heddle) and has a smooth-edged, round metal eye, is probably the best for handspun yarns.

Choose a **loom** that has a smooth shedding action rather than abrupt lifting action. Some looms have spring mechanisms that help to raise heavy shafts. But the shafts can pop up with surprising speed and abruptness. Cellulosic yarns are strong with a steadily applied load, but will snap with a sudden one.

Because flax and hemp are so inelastic, the optimal loom would have the breast and back beams separated by about 6 feet (1.8 m). Think about these inelastic yarns as if they were wire. Consider how little they stretch and how much effort it takes to open a shed. The greater the distance between the breast and back beams, the taller the shed through

HEDDLE TYPES

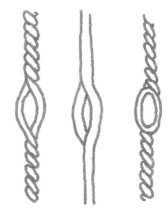

Left to right: **twisted wire heddle**, **flat steel heddle**, **inserted-eye heddle**.

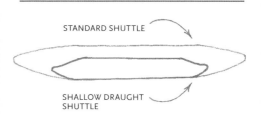

A shallow draught shuttle is about half the size of a standard shuttle and is ideal for narrow sheds.

which to pass a shuttle. However, not all of us have space for such a large loom. We need to accept the narrow shed and collect "shallow draught" shuttles.

A weight box filled with "odds and ends" permits ¼" to ½" (6 mm to 1.3 cm) advances in the warp.

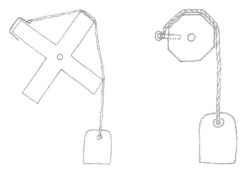

*The weight box can be attached to hooks in the cross arms of the **warp beam** (top) or hooked into holes drilled into **solid beams** (bottom).*

You can obtain a bigger shed if you remove or disable the brake on the warp beam and install a weight box—a long trough-like box filled with heavy odds and ends. With each change in tension as the shed opens and closes, the weight box "takes up the slack" and permits you to make ¼" to ½" (6 mm to 1.3 cm) advances in your warp, which helps to keep your selvedges even[30]. The weight box is tied to hooks attached to the cross arms of the warp beam (or hooked into holes drilled into solid beams). From time to time, you'll need to run to the back of the loom and lower and re-hang the weight box.

Take special care when winding the warp under tension. As you wind layer upon layer of warp on the warp beam, support each layer with packing sticks so that the layers remain separate (this will help maintain even tension). Be careful to spread the warp only as wide as the cloth width in the reed. Measure the width of the cloth at the reed and make sure that the warp is the same width over the back beam. No more. No less.

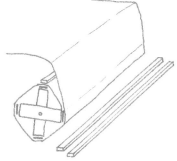

Support each layer of warp on the warp beam with packing sticks.

30 If you advance the warp in small increments, the arc of the weft is of more constant length. If you advance your warp every 4" (10 cm), the shuttle spills off significantly longer lengths at the onset. Those changes in weft length are reflected in the width of the cloth and warp tension at the selvedges.

Tips

❀ Start with a small project such as a stole, table runner, bag, placemats, dresser scarf, or belt. Likewise, use a narrow loom, if you have the choice.

❀ Avoid putting a narrow warp on a wide loom, such as an 8" (20.5 cm) wide warp on a 48" (122 cm) loom. Not all looms perform well in these circumstances. Centering the warp in the loom is a good start; however, doing so may not guarantee that this is the center of balance for each shaft. Thus, all shafts may not raise level with the same ease and may jam.

❀ Weave the bast fibers with a dampened weft. Plastic bobbins are handy; just dunk them in water with a drop of dish detergent. Squeeze excess water from the bobbin full of yarn, and you're ready to weave. You may also want to damp sponge the warp behind the castle. Wetting hemp and linen yarns softens them, lets the wefts pack, and makes the yarn stronger.

Handspun, handwoven hemp cloth has a "body" of its own.

Finishing the Cloth

AFTER YOU'VE REMOVED the cloth from the loom, boil the cloth to relax the structure, give it a better hand, remove soil from the spinning and weaving process, whiten it, and reduce raveling.[31]

Tie the warp ends near the fell edges and trim excess length off the warp yarns, unless you want fringe (singles do not make good fringe).

Fill a large soup or spaghetti pot (stainless steel, glass, or enamel over iron) with water. Make sure the pot has plenty of room for the fabric so that the cloth doesn't touch the bottom of the pot.

Add 2 tablespoons of washing soda, 1 tablespoon of household laundry detergent, then stir to dissolve the soap and soda.

Add your fabric, bring the contents to a simmer, and simmer for 30 to 45 minutes.

Turn off the heat and let the pot cool enough for you to dump the tea-colored soapy water down the drain.

Return the fabric to the pot and rinse in running water the temperature of a nice bath until the water is clear, the detergent is gone, and the fabric doesn't feel slippery.

If you intend to dye "in the cloth," it wouldn't hurt to boil linen or hemp cloth as above a couple more times to remove more gums, pectins, oils, and waxes. The bast fabrics will whiten some and you'll be rewarded with a better, clearer, more even dye job.

---

31 If you used milk or gelatin to size the yarn, then wash the fabric in warm, soapy water to remove the sizing before you boil the yarn. Rinse until the water runs clear.

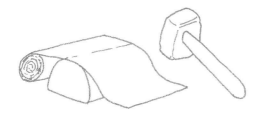

In beetling, dry fabric is placed on a smooth board and smacked with a smooth-faced mallet.

*The **beetled half** of this cloth (left) is smooth and shiny.*

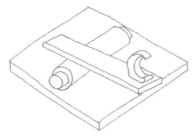

In mangling, a long flat board is drawn across dampened fabric that's been wound around a smooth wooden cylinder.

Beetling, Mangling, and Calendering Linen

Traditional linen weaving requires a final finishing technique to make the cloth more lustrous. In this final step, the linen cloth is pounded through beetling, mangling, or calendering.

In beetling, the dry fabric is placed on a smooth board and smacked with a smooth-faced mallet. The beetle mallet has rounded edges on the face that won't cut the yarns in the cloth, but rather squash them flat, to make the cloth shiny and help spread the yarns sideways to fill in small holes between the individual warp and weft yarns.

In mangling, the dampened fabric is wound onto a smooth wooden cylinder much like a jumbo rolling pin. Then a mangle—a long, flat board with a handle—is drawn across the fabric "sausage" with a firm downward pressure. This cold-press process rolls and compresses the fabric, making it smooth.

When this pressing job is assigned to a set of heavy hot steel rollers, it's a hot-press known as a calender. Calendering has the same effect of increasing the luster and closing the sett in the cloth.

Pressing with a steam iron also improves the appearance, smoothness, and luster of cotton, linen, and hemp fabrics.

Well, that about sums it up. My hope is that the foregoing has been useful and that soon your yarn baskets will be brimming. And may your friends happily wave at you with handspun, handwoven tea towels as they welcome you in for a cuppa!

Glossary of Terms

ACID An enemy of cellulose fibers. Common acids are acetic (vinegar), citric (oranges, lemons), phosphoric (soft drinks), and sulfuric (car batteries).

ALKALI An ally of cellulose fibers. Common household alkalis are ammonia, baking soda, washing soda, and lye.

BAST The spinning fibers found in the plant stem or trunk.

BATT A pillow of carded fiber from a bench, stock, or other carder.

BEETLE, BEETLING The act and process of pounding linen yarn and fabric to soften, smooth, and improve its luster.

BLEACH Bleaching can be destructive to cellulose fibers. Best whitening agents are soap, sunlight, and oxygen. The perborate bleaches are not as harmful. Chlorine bleaches are rough.

BOON The bits of plant core and straw that remain in hackled flax and hemp.

BREAK, BREAKING The tool and the process for crushing the core of retted bast fiber to begin separating textile fibers from the plant stem.

BROWN COTTON A natural-colored cotton. Cotton can be many colors such as green, buff, brown, red, chocolate. Often short stapled.

BUCKING The portion of the laundry process when cloth is soaked in mild alkali solution to remove grease, stains, and other tinges. It can whiten linen and hemp.

CALENDER A process that finishes fabric by pressure. It increases the luster and smoothness.

CALICO The original meaning was cloth from Calicut (Calcutta) in old India. Eighteenth-century calicoes were brilliantly colored, varied, and wonderful.

CANNABIS An ancient term for hemp. The genus of fiber- and resin-producing species of hemp.

CANVAS A firmly woven plain-weave cloth; from the original fiber's name, "cannabis."

CHARKHA Sanskrit for discus. Thus, "wheel" and "spinning wheel."

CHURGA In old India, a simple machine for removing cotton lint from the seeds; a gin.

COPP The wad of yarn built on the spindle blade (on a driven spindle) or shaft (on a hand spindle).

COTTON WEAVE Plain weave; tabby.

COUNT SYSTEM An indirect measurement system based on the number of skeins of a given length to weigh a pound. The count systems were specific to fiber as well as locales. A 1-count cotton is 840 yards per pound. A 2-count cotton is 1,680 yards per pound, and so forth. A 1-count linen yarn is 300 yards per pound. A 1-count hemp yarn is often 840 yards per pound.

CROFTING A method of bleaching linen fabric by laying it out in the field to bleach by sunlight and contact with green grasses (oxygen source).

DACCA MUSLIN An ancient cotton fabric from Dacca, India. A treasure of extreme fineness, nearly invisible when wetted.

DAMASK A figured cloth, often linen, later cotton, based on satin weave.

DECORTICATE A process that removes bast fibers from the stem by scraping.

DENIM A sturdy cotton cloth woven in a 2/1 twill; a specialty of Nimes, France, known as "serge de Nimes," thus "denim."

DETERGENT In this context, a cleanser (e.g., Tide, Cheer) that we use when washing cloth items; all (without bleach or optical brighteners) work well on cellulosic fibers. But good old-fashioned soap and hot soft water are the best.

DIAPER A linen, and later a cotton cloth, with a diamond figure; from "clothe d'Ypres." Ypres was a linen center in medieval Flanders.

DIRECT DYES Synthetic dyes with weak bonds used on cellulosic yarns. Colors are classic 1950s chocolate, yellow-greens, orangey-reds. Good lightfastness. Weak washfastness.

DRAFT The fiber attenuation or "drawing out" process (both verb and noun).

DRAFTING ZONE The area (triangular and the length of the fiber staple) where loose fiber is drawn into yarn; it has twist on one end, loose fiber on the other.

DRIFT A yarn defect. When under tension, the yarn slips or "drifts" apart, drafting itself to nothing. Caused by not enough twist.

END In weaving, a warp end, one of many in a warp.

FIMBLE "Fimble hemp" is an ancient term for fiber from the male hemp plant.

FINGER A portion of the flax strick.

GIN An English contraction of archaic "engine"; other forms are "jenny," "jinny," and "jimmy." For our purpose, it means the device used to separate cotton fiber from the seed.

GOSSYPIUM A member of the mallow plant family, related to hollyhocks and okra, commonly known as cotton.

GOSSYPOL A toxic component of the cotton plant and seed.

GRASSING A bleaching process (same as "crofting") for linen cloth: spreading the fabric out in sunlight on green grasses to bleach by ultraviolet light and oxygen from the undergrowth.

GRIST An old word that describes all that's necessary to make a yarn. More recently, it focuses on a length/weight ratio: usually expressed as "yards per pound" or "meters per kilo."

HACKLE, HECKLE, HETCHELL A process and device for separating line flax fibers: bundled fibers, after being broken and scutched, are drawn through the hackle, a sturdy block with pointed spikes.

HANK A skein and, in old count systems, a skein of a given length. In the cotton system, a hank of cotton contains 840 yards (768 m). In the linen system, a hank (lea) contains 300 yards (274 m).

HURDS The bits of pith and interior core that remain on hemp fiber after hackling.

JEANS A term from "Genoas," sixteenth-century Genoese sailors who favored durable comfortable trousers, made from cloth of Nimes.

JOINS The various techniques that connect unspun fiber to yarn so that it holds together invisibly. A strong, dependable join should be drafted.

KNOP YARN A novelty yarn consisting of a core yarn plied with a second yarn that wraps back on itself at intervals forming lumps or "knops."

LAP A tissue of open carded fiber right off the handcard.

LEA A unit of the linen count system; each skein was a "lea" of 300 yards (274 m).

LEAF TRASH The bits of cotton leaves introduced when cotton lint is picked. The amount of leaf trash affects the grade of cotton.

LINACEAE The flax plant family. *Linum usitatissimum* is the fiber flax.

LINE A flax fiber form, encompassing fiber from roots to the flower. As opposed to "tow."

LINSEED OIL Also called flaxseed oil, it has many uses, from paints and finishes to linoleum, oil cloth, and food supplements.

LINEN The yarn and fabric made from flax. Historically, it's more a term of usage than a specific fiber. Several bast fibers (hops, nettle, flax, hemp) yarns and fabric were called "linen."

LINT The generic name for cotton fiber in the fluff form, the cotton version of "fleece."

MANGLE To flatten and make lustrous a bast fabric by cool pressing; also, the device that performs this process.

MERCERIZING After John Mercer (c. 1844): a process of wetting cotton cloth or yarn in strong alkali solution. It has the remarkable effect of popping open the cotton fiber core that had collapsed with natural drying. This slack mercerization makes the yarn 40% stronger. However, perle cotton is extended while in caustic solution, which improves the luster but diminishes the fiber strength.

MORDANT A chemical assist (metallic salt) used to help dyestuffs "lock-on" to the fiber molecules.

MORDANT DYES Also called "natural" or plant-source dyes, they're applied to cotton, linen, silk, and wool. When used without a mordant, the colors are lighter, softer, and are less washfast.

MOTES The immature seeds, or bits of seed hull included in ginned cotton. They contain tannin and can dye the cotton yarn a manila color.

NAP A furred or hairy surface on cloth made by construction, as in velvet, or raised after weaving by brushing.

NEPS The tangles or knots of cotton fiber that can't be carded out. They cause slubby yarn.

NODES The swelling at intervals along a plant fiber. In the case of flax, the node looks like miniature bamboo. In cotton, it's the point at which the spiral growth reverses direction.

OXFORD WEAVE A traditional and excellent weave for cotton garment cloth; an extended plain weave made up of paired warp ends and single weft picks.

PACKING STICKS In weaving, the sticks, rods, or dowels used while beaming the warp to keep discrete layers on the warp beam.

PHLOEM The cell structures in plant stems or trunks that transfer food between roots and leaves. A source for bast spinning fiber.

PICK In weaving, the weft yarn and its passage through the shed. Also, a "shot."

PITH The soft spongy tissue found in the core of hemp and surrounding the hollow core of flax.

PUNI A dense small rolag-like form of cotton fiber preparation. Works well with short-stapled cottons. Fiber is ginned, then bowed or carded before being rolled up into punis. Possibly from Sanskrit.

RAYON The generic name for regenerated cellulose from a variety of plant sources.

REACTIVE DYES Also known as "fiber reactive" dyes. Modern synthetic dyestuffs with good bonding power used on cellulose fibers. Their palette is broad: bright clear colors, red/blue/yellow, cyan/magenta/yellow. Most are washfast and lightfast.

RET A moist, selective decomposition, rot.

RIPPLE A rake-like device used to "comb" the seeds out of dried flax straw.

ROLAG A fiber form made from a carded lap that has been rolled up.

ROVING A fine-diameter, open, untwisted ribbon of fibers. Also known as pencil roving.

SCOUR Rigorous washing to remove greases, waxes, and soil.

SCUTCH The process that removes broken pith and core from hackled flax and hemp.

SCUTCHING SWORD, STAKE A handheld wooden knife and board or stake used to separate boon from flax or hemp without breaking the long fiber.

SEED FIBERS Cotton, kapok, and coir.

SHEAVES, SHOCKS, SHOVES, SPRATS, STOOKS All are terms for cut bundles of flax or hemp left to dry in the field.

SHIVES In flax, the broken pith and core material; a lot of it is removed with breaking and scutching.

SIZING A temporary glue or paste applied to warp yarns to aid in the weaving process with the aim to control fuzz, lively twist, and to assist in threading the loom.

SKEIN A yarn wound into a circle and tied in several places. Also, a hank.

SLIVER Similar to roving, except fairly dense and large in diameter.

SNUB In this context, to restrict movement.

SOAP The product of a complex reaction between alkali solutions and fats or oils.

STAPLE An old word, originally noun and verb, to describe and determine fiber length.

STRICK A bundle of line flax or hemp.

TAKE-UP The strength and speed with which yarn is drawn onto the bobbin.

TAHKLI A small supported spindle with a point on each tip (Urdu).

TOW The shorter fiber left on the hackles after processing line flax and hemp.

T.P.I. The abbreviation for "turns per inch," a measurement of twist.

ULTIMATES The building-block cells in flax fiber. They are spindle shaped and longer than 1" (2.5 cm).

VAT DYES Dyestuffs characterized by insolubility, crystalline structure, and good light- and washfastness. Indigo, woad, and Imperial Purple (murex) are vat dyes of antiquity. Because no chemical bonding occurs, but rather physical embedding, one may argue that vat dyes are pigments.

WEIGHT BOX In weaving, a box under the warp beam that serves to tension the warp while weaving. It replaces a ratchet system.

WINNOW To separate seed hull or chaff from the seed.

XYLEM The water-transport cells found in plant stems/ trunks.

Y.P.P., YDS/LB Abbreviations for "yards per pound," a primary grist measurement.

Selected Bibliography

Amos, Alden. *The Alden Amos Big Book of Handspinning: Being a Compendium of Information, Advice, and Opinions on the Noble Art & Craft*. Loveland, Colorado: Interweave, 2001.

Ashenhurst, Thos. R. *A treatise on textile calculawtions and the structure of fabrics*. Huddersfield: Broadbent, 1902.

Baines, Patricia. *Linen: Hand Spinning and Weaving*. Loveland, Colorado: Interweave, 1989.

Boyce, S.S. *Hemp: A Practical Treatise on the Culture of Hemp for Seed and Fiber with a Sketch of the History and Nature of the Hemp Plant*. New York: Orange Judd, 1912.

Bradbury, F. *Calculations in Yarns and Fabrics*. Manchester, England: Emmot & Company, 1920.

Bradbury, Fred. *Flax Culture and Preparation*, London: I. Pitman, 1920.

Hamby, Dame Scott. *The American Cotton Handbook*. New York: Interscience, 1965.

Hamilton, Roy W, B., Lynne Milgram, Sylvia Fraser-Lu, and Fowler Museum at UCLA. *Material Choices: Refashioning Bast and Leaf Fibers in Asia and the Pacific*. Los Angeles: Fowler Museum at UCLA, 2007.

Heinrich, Linda. *The Magic of Linen: Flax Seed to Woven Cloth*. Victoria, British Columbia: Orca, 1992.

———. 2010. *Linen: From Flax Seed to Woven Cloth*. Atglen, Pennsylvania: Schiffer, 2010.

Hochberg, Bette. Reprints of Bette Hochberg's textile articles. Santa Cruz, California; Berkeley, California: Bette Hochberg, 1982 (available through Textile Artists' Supply).

Horner, John. *The Linen Trade of Europe During the Spinning-Wheel Period*. Belfast: M'Caw, Stevenson & Orr, 1920.

Linder, Olive, and Harry P. Linder. *Handspinning Flax*. Phoenix, Arizona: Bizarre Butterfly, 1986.

Linder, Olive, Harry P. Linder, and Roberta Sinnock. *Hand Spinning Cotton*. Phoenix, Arizona: Cotton Squares, 1977.

Matthews, J. Merritt. *The Textile Fibres: Their Physical, Microscopical and Chemical Properties*. New York: J. Wiley & Sons, 1916.

Mejía de Rodas, Idalma, Linda Asturias de Barrios, and Museo Ixchel del Traje Indígena de Guatemala. *Cuyuscate: Brown Cotton in the Textile Tradition of Guatemala*. Guatemala: Museo Ixchel del Traje Indígena, 2002.

Stark, Les. *Hempstone Heritage I: In Accordance With Their Wills: "All the Heckled Hemp She Can Spin."* Ephrata, Pennsylvania: Hempstone Heritage, 2005.

Worst, Edward F. *How to Weave Linens*. Milwaukee, Wisconsin: Bruce Publishing, 1926.

Sett Table Ashenhurst Formula Chart for Setts

GRIST	SETT FOR TABBY	SETT FOR 2/2 TWILL	GRIST	SETT FOR TABBY	SETT FOR 2/2 TWILL	GRIST	SETT FOR TABBY	SETT FOR 2/2 TWILL
(YD/LB)	(EPI)	(EPI)	(YD/LB)	(EPI)	(EPI)	(YD/LB)	(EPI)	(EPI)
1000	10.12	13.49	3400	18.66	24.88	5800	24.37	32.49
1100	10.61	14.15	3500	18.93	25.24	5900	24.58	32.77
1200	11.09	14.78	3600	19.2	25.6	6000	24.79	33.05
1300	11.54	15.88	3700	19.46	25.95	6100	24.99	33.32
1400	11.97	15.96	3800	19.73	26.3	6200	25.2	33.6
1500	12.39	16.52	3900	19.98	26.65	6300	25.4	33.87
1600	12.8	17.06	4000	20.24	26.98	6400	25.6	34.13
1700	13.19	17.59	4100	20.49	27.31	6500	25.8	34.4
1800	13.58	18.10	4200	20.74	27.65	6600	26	34.66
1900	13.95	18.59	4300	20.98	27.98	6700	26.19	34.92
2000	14.31	19.08	4400	21.23	28.30	6800	26.39	35.18
2100	14.66	19.55	4500	21.47	28.62	6900	26.58	35.44
2200	15.01	20.01	4600	21.7	28.54	7000	26.77	35.7
2300	15.35	20.46	4700	21.94	29.25	7100	26.96	35.95
2400	15.68	20.90	4800	22.17	29.56	7200	27.15	36.2
2500	16	21.33	4900	22.4	29.87	7300	27.34	36.45
2600	16.32	21.75	5000	22.63	30.17	7400	27.53	36.7
2700	16.63	22.17	5100	22.85	30.47	7500	27.71	36.95
2800	16.93	22.57	5200	23.08	30.77	7600	27.9	37.2
2900	17.23	22.97	5300	23.3	31.06	7700	28.08	37.44
3000	17.53	23.39	5400	23.52	31.35	7800	28.26	37.68
3100	17.82	23.76	5500	23.73	31.64	7900	28.44	37.92
3200	18.1	24.14	5600	23.95	31.92	8000	28.62	38.16
3300	18.38	24.51	5700	24.16	32.21	8100	28.8	38.4

GRIST	SETT FOR TABBY	SETT FOR 2/2 TWILL
(YD/LB)	(EPI)	(EPI)
8200	28.98	38.4
8300	29.15	39.87
8400	29.33	39.10
8500	29.5	39.34
8600	29.68	39.57
8700	29.84	39.8
8800	30.02	40.02
8900	30.19	40.25
9000	30.36	40.7
9100	30.53	40.7
9200	30.69	40.92
9300	30.86	41.15
9400	31.03	41.37
9500	31.19	41.59
9600	31.35	41.80
9700	31.52	42.02
9800	31.68	42.24
9900	31.84	42.45
10000	32	42.67
12500	35.78	47.7
15000	39.19	52.26
17500	42.33	56.44
20000	45.25	60.34

The Ashenhurst Formula is based on using identical warp and weft yarns. The numbers here have already been factored for hobby looms and medium soft yarns. Round up for worsted or lean yarns; otherwise, round down.

The original formula is based on the yarn diameter, the number of ends per pattern repeat, and the number of intersections per pattern repeat.

NUMBER OF YARN DIAMETERS PER INCH: the total number of yarns that can be squashed into 1" (2.5 cm). Or you can get this number by taking the square root of the grist of your yarn in yd/lb. (Three cheers for pocket calculators!)

This number has been factored for softness by multiplying it by 0.8 as the numbers are entered into the formula.

NUMBER OF ENDS PER REPEAT: the number of warps in each pattern repeat; 2/2 twill, for example, has 4 ends per repeat.

NUMBER OF INTERSECTIONS PER REPEAT: the number of times the weft passes from back to face, or face to back of the cloth in each pattern repeat. Minimum number is 2.

Sett = [(number of yarn diameters per inch) × (number of ends per repeat)] ÷ (number of ends per repeat + number of intersections per repeat)

The end "sett" has been factored for our hobby looms and shuttles by multiplying this number by 0.8 at the end of the calculation.

Index

Enhance your *spinning experience* & create *beautiful yarns* with these how-to resources from Interweave

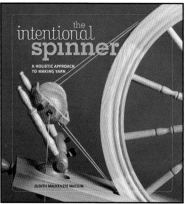

Spin Art
Mastering the Craft of Spinning Textured Yarn
Jacey Boggs
ISBN 978-1-59668-362-4
$26.95

The Intentional Spinner
A Holistic Approach to Making Yarn
Judith MacKenzie McCuin
ISBN 978-1-59668-080-7
$26.95

Respect the Spindle
Spin Infinite Yarns with One Amazing Tool
Abby Franquemont
ISBN 978-1-59668-155-2
$22.95

Available at your favorite retailer or

shop.spinningdaily.com

The magazine that highlights the vibrant and diverse spinning community and explores the intricacies of the craft. *Spinoffmagazine.com*

Join the online community just for spinners! You'll get a free eNewsletter, free patterns, pattern store, blogs, event updates, galleries, tips and techniques, and much more! Sign up at *Spinningdaily.com*